THE MANDALAY EDITION OF THE WORKS OF RUDYARD KIPLING

SONGS FROM BOOKS

THE YEARS BETWEEN
AND PARODIES

BY

RUDYARD KIPLING

GARDEN CITY   NEW YORK
DOUBLEDAY, PAGE & COMPANY
1925

PRINTED IN THE UNITED STATES
AT
THE COUNTRY LIFE PRESS, GARDEN CITY, N. Y.

PREFACE

I HAVE collected in this volume practically all the verses and chapter-headings scattered through my books. In several cases where only a few lines of verse were originally used, I have given in full the song, etc., from which they were taken.

I wish to acknowledge the courtesy of the Clarendon Press in allowing me to print my verses from the 'School History of England.'

8571

CONTENTS

SONGS FROM BOOKS

CONTENTS

SONGS FROM BOOKS

CONTENTS

SONGS FROM BOOKS

CONTENTS

SONGS FROM BOOKS

CONTENTS

INDEX TO FIRST LINES

SONGS FROM BOOKS

INDEX TO FIRST LINES

SONGS FROM BOOKS

INDEX TO FIRST LINES

SONGS FROM BOOKS

INDEX TO FIRST LINES

SONGS FROM BOOKS

SONGS FROM BOOKS

CITIES AND THRONES AND POWERS

CITIES and Thrones and Powers,
 Stand in Time's eye,
Almost as long as flowers,
 Which daily die;
But, as new buds put forth
 To glad new men,
Out of the spent and unconsidered Earth
 The Cities rise again.

This season's Daffodil,
 She never hears,
What change, what chance, what chill,
 Cut down last year's:
But with bold countenance,
 And knowledge small,
Esteems her seven days' continuance,
 To be perpetual.

So Time that is o'er-kind,
 To all that be,
Ordains us e'en as blind,
 As bold as she:
That in our very death,
 And burial sure,
Shadow to shadow, well-persuaded, saith,
 'See how our works endure!'

THE RECALL

I AM the land of their fathers.
    In me the virtue stays.
    I will bring back my children,
    After certain days.

Under their feet in the grasses
    My clinging magic runs.
They shall return as strangers,
    They shall remain as sons.

Over their heads in the branches
    Of their new-bought, ancient trees,
I weave an incantation
    And draw them to my knees.

Scent of smoke in the evening,
    Smell of rain in the night,
The hours, the days and the seasons,
    Order their souls aright;

Till I make plain the meaning
    Of all my thousand years—
Till I fill their hearts with knowledge,
    While I fill their eyes with tears.

THE CENTURION'S SONG

LEGATE, I had the news last night—my cohort ordered
        home
    By ship to Portus Itius and thence by road to
        Rome.
I've marched the companies aboard, the arms are stowed
    below:
Now let another take my sword.   Command me not to
    go!

I've served in Britain forty years, from Vectis to the
    Wall,
I have none other home than this, nor any life at all.
Last night I did not understand, but, now the hour draws
    near
That calls me to my native land, I feel that land is here.

Here where, men say, my name was made, here where
    my work was done,
Here where my dearest dead are laid—my wife—my
    wife and son
Here where time, custom, grief and toil, age, memory,
    service, love,
Have rooted me in British soil.   Ah, how shall I re-
    move?

5

For me this land, that sea, these airs, those folk and
    fields suffice.
What purple Southern pomp can match our changeful
    Northern skies,
Black with December snows unshed or pearled with
    August haze,
The clanging arch of steel-gray March, or June's long-
    lighted days?

You'll follow widening Rhodanus till vine and olive lean
Aslant before the sunny breeze that sweeps Nemausus
    clean
To Arelate's triple gate; but let me linger on,
Here where our stiff-necked British oaks confront Eur-
    oclydon!

You'll take the old Aurelian Road through shore-
    descending pines
Where, blue as any peacock's neck, the Tyrrhene Ocean
    shines.
You'll go where laurel crowns are won, but will you e'er
    forget
The scent of hawthorn in the sun, or bracken in the wet?

Let me work here for Britain's sake—at any task you
    will—
A marsh to drain, a road to make or native troops to
    drill.
Some Western camp (I know the Pict) or granite Border
    keep,
Mid seas of heather derelict, where our old messmates
    sleep.

THE CENTURION'S SONG

Legate, I come to you in tears—My cohort ordered
    home!
I've served in Britain forty years. What should I do
    in Rome?
Here is my heart, my soul, my mind—the only life I
    know.—
I cannot leave it all behind. Command me not to go!

PUCK'S SONG

SEE you the ferny ride that steals
    Into the oak-woods far?
  O that was whence they hewed the keels
    That rolled to Trafalgar.

And mark you where the ivy clings
    To Bayham's mouldering walls?
O there we cast the stout railings
    That stand around St. Paul's.

See you the dimpled track that runs
    All hollow through the wheat?
O that was where they hauled the guns
    That smote King Philip's fleet.

Out of the Weald, the secret Weald,
    Men sent in ancient years,
The horse-shoes red at Flodden Field,
    The arrows at Poitiers.

See you our little mill that clacks,
    So busy by the brook?
She has ground her corn and paid her tax
    Ever since Domesday Book.

PUCK'S SONG

See you our stilly woods of oak?
  And the dread ditch beside?
O that was where the Saxons broke
  On the day that Harold died.

See you the windy levels spread
  About the gates of Rye?
O that was where the Northmen fled,
  When Alfred's ships came by.

See you our pastures wide and lone,
  Where the red oxen browse?
O there was a City thronged and known,
  Ere London boasted a house.

And see you, after rain, the trace
  Of mound and ditch and wall?
O that was a Legion's camping-place,
  When Cæsar sailed from Gaul.

And see you marks that show and fade,
  Like shadows on the Downs?
O they are the lines the Flint Men made,
  To guard their wondrous towns.

Trackway and Camp and City lost,
  Salt Marsh where now is corn;
Old Wars, old Peace, old Arts that cease,
  And so was England born!

She is not any common Earth,
  Water or wood or air,
But Merlin's Isle of Gramarye,
  Where you and I will fare.

THE WAY THROUGH THE WOODS

THEY shut the road through the woods
    Seventy years ago.
    Weather and rain have undone it again,
    And now you would never know
There was once a road through the woods
  Before they planted the trees.
It is underneath the coppice and heath,
  And the thin anemones.
  Only the keeper sees
That, where the ring-dove broods,
  And the badgers roll at ease,
There was once a road through the woods.

Yet, if you enter the woods
  Of a summer evening late,
When the night-air cools on the trout-ringed pools
  Where the otter whistles his mate
(They fear not men in the woods,
  Because they see so few),
You will hear the beat of a horse's feet,
  And the swish of a skirt in the dew,
  Steadily cantering through
The misty solitudes,
  As though they perfectly knew
The old lost road through the woods . . .
But there is no road through the woods.

A THREE-PART SONG

I'M just in love with all these three,
   The Weald and the Marsh and the Down countrie;
   Nor I don't know which I love the most,
The Weald or the Marsh or the white chalk coast!

I've buried my heart in a ferny hill,
Twix' a liddle low shaw an' a great high gill.
Oh hop-bine yaller an' wood-smoke blue,
I reckon you'll keep her middling true!

I've loosed my mind for to out and run
On a Marsh that was old when Kings begun.
Oh Romney Level and Brenzett reeds,
I reckon you know what my mind needs!

I've given my soul to the Southdown grass,
And sheep-bells tinkled where you pass.
Oh Firle an' Ditchling an' sails at sea,
I reckon you keep my soul for me!

THE RUN OF THE DOWNS

THE Weald is good, the Downs are best—
I'll give you the run of 'em, East to West.
Beachy Head and Winddoor Hill,
They were once and they are still,
Firle, Mount Caburn and Mount Harry
Go back as far as sums'll carry.
Ditchling Beacon and Chanctonbury Ring,
They have looked on many a thing,
And what those two have missed between 'em
I reckon Truleigh Hill has seen 'em.
Highden, Bignor and Duncton Down
Knew Old England before the Crown.
Linch Down, Treyford and Sunwood
Knew Old England before the Flood.
And when you end on the Hampshire side—
Butser's old as Time and Tide.

The Downs are sheep, the Weald is corn,
You be glad you are Sussex born!

BROOKLAND ROAD

I WAS very well pleased with what I knowed,
   I reckoned myself no fool—
Till I met with a maid on the Brookland Road,
   That turned me back to school.

  Low down—low down!
    Where the liddle green lanterns shine—
  O maids, I've done with 'ee all but one,
    And she can never be mine!

'Twas right in the middest of a hot June night,
   With thunder duntin' round,
And I see'd her face by the fairy light
   That beats from off the ground.

She only smiled and she never spoke,
   She smiled and went away;
But when she'd gone my heart was broke
   And my wits was clean astray.

O, stop your ringing and let me be—
   Let be, O Brookland bells!
You'll ring Old Goodman[1] out of the sea,
   Before I wed one else!

[1] Earl Godwin of the Goodwin Sands?

Old Goodman's Farm is rank sea sand,
  And was this thousand year;
But it shall turn to rich plough land
  Before I change my dear.

O, Fairfield Church is water-bound
  From autumn to the spring;
But it shall turn to high hill ground
  Before my bells do ring.

O, leave me walk on the Brookland Road,
  In the thunder and warm rain—
O, leave me look where my love goed,
  And p'raps I'll see her again!

    Low down—low down!
      Where the liddle green lanterns shine—
    O maids, I've done with 'ee all but one,
      And she can never be mine!

THE SACK OF THE GODS

STRANGERS drawn from the ends of the earth,
    jewelled and plumed were we;
    I was Lord of the Inca race, and she was Queen
    of the Sea.
Under the stars beyond our stars where the new-forged
    meteors glow,
Hotly we stormed Valhalla, a million years ago.

Ever 'neath high Valhalla Hall the well-tuned horns begin
When the swords are out in the underworld, and the
    weary Gods come in.
Ever through high Valhalla Gate the Patient Angel goes,
He opens the eyes that are blind with hate—he joins the
    hands of foes.

Dust of the stars was under our feet, glitter of stars
    above—
Wrecks of our wrath dropped reeling down as we fought
    and we spurned and we strove.
Worlds upon worlds we tossed aside, and scattered them
    to and fro,
The night that we stormed Valhalla, a million years ago!

They are forgiven as they forgive all those dark wounds
    and deep,
Their beds are made on the lap of Time and they lie
    down and sleep.

15

They are forgiven as they forgive all those old wounds
that bleed,
They shut their eyes from their worshippers. They
sleep till the world has need.

She with the star I had marked for my own—I with my
set desire—
Lost in the loom of the Night of Nights—lighted by
worlds afire—
Met in a war against the Gods where the headlong me-
teors glow,
Hewing our way to Valhalla, a million years ago!

They will come back—come back again, as long as the
red Earth rolls.
He never wasted a leaf or a tree. Do you think He
would squander souls?

THE KINGDOM

NOW we are come to our Kingdom,
    And the State is thus and thus;
Our legions wait at the Palace gate—
    Little it profits us,
        Now we are come to our Kingdom!

Now we are come to our Kingdom,
    And the Crown is ours to take—
With a naked sword at the Council board,
    And under the throne the snake,
        Now we are come to our Kingdom!

Now we are come to our Kingdom,
    And the Realm is ours by right,
With shame and fear for our daily cheer,
    And heaviness at night,
        Now we are come to our Kingdom!

Now we are come to our Kingdom,
    But my love's eyelids fall.
All that I wrought for, all that I fought for,
    Delight her nothing at all.
My crown is of withered leaves,
For she sits in the dust and grieves,
        Now we are come to our Kingdom!

17

TARRANT MOSS

I CLOSED and drew for my love's sake
  That now is false to me,
And I slew the Reiver of Tarrant Moss
  And set Dumeny free.

They have gone down, they have gone down,
  They are standing all arow—
Twenty knights in the peat-water,
  That never struck a blow!

Their armour shall not dull nor rust,
  Their flesh shall not decay,
For Tarrant Moss holds them in trust,
  Until the Judgment Day.

Their soul went from them in their youth,
  Ah God, that mine had gone,
Whenas I leaned on my love's truth
  And not on my sword alone!

Whenas I leaned on lad's belief
  And not on my naked blade—
And I slew a thief, and an honest thief,
  For the sake of a worthless maid.

18

TARRANT MOSS

They have laid the Reiver low in his place,
    They have set me up on high,
But the twenty knights in the peat-water
    Are luckier than I.

And ever they give me gold and praise
    And ever I mourn my loss—
For I struck the blow for my false love's sake
    And not for the Men of the Moss!

WILLIAM THE CONQUEROR'S SONG

ENGLAND'S on the anvil—hear the hammers
     ring—
     Clanging from the Severn to the Tyne!
Never was a blacksmith like our Norman King—
     England's being hammered, hammered, ham-
     mered into line!

England's on the anvil!   Heavy are the blows!
     (But the work will be a marvel when it's done)
Little bits of Kingdoms cannot stand against their foes.
     England's being hammered, hammered, ham-
     mered into one!

There shall be one people—it shall serve one Lord—
     (Neither Priest nor Baron shall escape!)
It shall have one speech and law, soul and strength and
     sword.
     England's being hammered, hammered, ham-
     mered into shape!

SIR RICHARD'S SONG

(A.D. 1066)

I FOLLOWED my Duke ere I was a lover,
    To take from England fief and fee;
But now this game is the other way over—
    But now England hath taken me!

I had my horse, my shield and banner,
    And a boy's heart, so whole and free;
But now I sing in another manner—
    But now England hath taken me!

As for my Father in his tower,
    Asking news of my ship at sea;
He will remember his own hour—
    Tell him England hath taken me!

As for my Mother in her bower,
    That rules my Father so cunningly,
She will remember a maiden's power—
    Tell her England hath taken me!

As for my Brother in Rouen City,
    A nimble and naughty page is he,
But he will come to suffer and pity—
    Tell him England hath taken me!

As for my little Sister waiting
  In the pleasant orchards of Normandie,
Tell her youth is the time for mating—
  Tell her England hath taken me!

As for my Comrades in camp and highway,
  That lift their eyebrows scornfully,
Tell them their way is not my way—
  Tell them England hath taken me!

Kings and Princes and Barons famed,
  Knights and Captains in your degree;
Hear me a little before I am blamed—
  Seeing England hath taken me!

Howso great man's strength be reckoned,
  There are two things he cannot flee;
Love is the first, and Death is the second—
  And Love in England hath taken me!

THE NORMAN BARON

(A. D. 1100)

'MY son,' said the Norman Baron, 'I am dying, and
you will be heir
To all the broad acres in England that William
gave me for my share
When we conquered the Saxon at Hastings, and a nice
little handful it is.
But before you go over to rule it I want you to understand this:—

'The Saxon is not like us Normans. His manners are
not so polite,
But he never means anything serious till he talks about
justice and right;
When he stands like an ox in the furrow with his sullen
set eyes on your own,
And grumbles, "This isn't fair dealing," my son, leave
the Saxon alone.

'You can horsewhip your Gascony archers, or torture
your Picardy spears,
But don't try that game on the Saxon—you'll have the
whole brood round your ears!
23

From the richest old Thane in the county to the poorest
    chained serf in the fields,
They'll be at you and on you like hornets, and, if you
    are wise, you will yield!

'But first you must master their language, their dialect,
    proverbs and songs,
Don't trust any clerk to interpret when they come with
    the tale of their wrongs.
Let them know that you know what they're saying; let
    them feel that you know what to say;
Yes, even when you want to go hunting, hear them out
    if it takes you all day.

'They'll drink every hour of the daylight and poach
    every hour of the dark,
It's the sport not the rabbits they're after (we've plenty
    of game in the park).
Don't hang them or cut off their fingers. That's waste-
    ful as well as unkind,
For a hard-bitten, South-country poacher makes the
    best man-at-arms you can find.

'Appear with your wife and the children at their wed-
    dings and funerals and feasts;
Be polite but not friendly to Bishops; be good to all
    poor parish-priests;
Say "we," "us" and "ours" when you're talking in-
    stead of "you fellows" and "I."
Don't ride over seeds; keep your temper; and never you
    tell 'em a lie!'

24

A TREE SONG

(A. D. 1200)

O F all the trees that grow so fair,
  Old England to adorn,
    Greater are none beneath the Sun,
      Than Oak, and Ash, and Thorn.
Sing Oak, and Ash, and Thorn, good sirs
  (All of a Midsummer morn!)
Surely we sing no little thing,
  In Oak, and Ash, and Thorn!

Oak of the Clay lived many a day
  Or ever Æneas began;
Ash of the Loam was a lady at home
  When Brut was an outlaw man.
Thorn of the Down saw New Troy Town
  (From which was London born);
Witness hereby the ancientry
  Of Oak, and Ash, and Thorn!

Yew that is old in churchyard mould,
  He breedeth a mighty bow.
Alder for shoes do wise men choose,
  And beech for cups also.

But when ye have killed, and your bowl is spilled,
  And your shoes are clean outworn,
Back ye must speed for all that ye need,
  To Oak, and Ash, and Thorn!

Ellum she hateth mankind, and waiteth
  Till every gust be laid,
To drop a limb on the head of him
  That anyway trusts her shade:
But whether a lad be sober or sad,
  Or mellow with ale from the horn,
He will take no wrong when he lieth along
  'Neath Oak, and Ash, and Thorn!

Oh, do not tell the Priest our plight,
  Or he would call it a sin;
But—we have been out in the woods all night,
  A-conjuring Summer in!
And we bring you news by word of mouth—
  Good news for cattle and corn—
Now is the Sun come up from the South,
  With Oak, and Ash, and Thorn!

Sing Oak, and Ash, and Thorn, good sirs
  (All of a Midsummer morn!)
England shall bide till Judgment Tide,
  By Oak, and Ash, and Thorn!

OLD MOTHER LAIDINWOOL

OLD Mother Laidinwool had nigh twelve months been dead.
  She heard the hops was doing well an' so popped up her head,
For she said:—'The lads I've picked with when I was young and fair,
They're bound to be at hopping and I'm bound to meet 'em there!'

  Let me up and go
  Back to the work I know, Lord!
  Back to the work I know, Lord!
  For it's dark where I lie down, My Lord!
  An' it's dark where I lie down!

Old Mother Laidinwool, she give her bones a shake,
An' trotted down the churchyard path as fast as she could make.
She met the Parson walking, but she says to him, says she:—
'Oh don't let no one trouble for a poor old ghost like me!'

'Twas all a warm September an' the hops had flourished grand,
She saw the folks get into 'em with stockin's on their hands;

27

An' none of 'em was foreigners but all which she ha
    known,
And old Mother Laidinwool she blessed 'em every one

She saw her daughters picking an' their childern then
    beside,
An' she moved among the babies an' she stilled 'em
    when they cried.
She saw their clothes was bought not begged, an' they
    was clean an' fat,
An' Old Mother Laidinwool she thanked the Lord for
    that.

Old Mother Laidinwool she waited on all day
Until it come too dark to see an' people went away—
Until it come too dark to see an' lights began to show,
An' old Mother Laidinwool she hadn't where to go.

Old Mother Laidinwool she give her bones a shake,
An' trotted back to churchyard-mould as fast as she
    could make.
She went where she was bidden to an' there laid down
    her ghost, . . .
An' the Lord have mercy on you in the Day you need it
    most!

      Let me in again,
      Out of the wet an' rain, Lord!
      Out of the dark an' rain, Lord!
      For it's best as you shall say, My Lord!
      An' it's best as you shall say!

CUCKOO SONG

(Spring begins in Southern England on the 14th April,
on which date the Old Woman lets the Cuckoo out of
her basket at Heathfield Fair—locally known as Heffle
Cuckoo Fair.)

TELL it to the locked-up trees,
    Cuckoo, bring your song here!
    Warrant, Act and Summons, please,
      For Spring to pass along here!
Tell old Winter, if he doubt,
  Tell him squat and square—a!
Old Woman!
Old Woman!
Old Woman's let the Cuckoo out
  At Heffle Cuckoo Fair—a!

March has searched and April tried—
  'Tisn't long to May now.
Not so far to Whitsuntide
  And Cuckoo's come to stay now!
Hear the valiant fellow shout
  Down the orchard bare—a!
Old Woman!
Old Woman!
Old Woman's let the Cuckoo out
  At Heffle Cuckoo Fair—a!

29

When your heart is young and gay
   And the season rules it—
Work your works and play your play
   'Fore the Autumn cools it!
Kiss you turn and turn about,
   But my lad, beware—a!
Old Woman!
Old Woman!
Old Woman's let the Cuckoo out
   At Heffle Cuckoo Fair—a!

A CHARM

TAKE of English earth as much
　　As either hand may rightly clutch.
　　In the taking of it breathe
Prayer for all who lie beneath.
Not the great nor well-bespoke,
But the mere uncounted folk
Of whose life and death is none
Report or lamentation.
　　Lay that earth upon thy heart,
　　And thy sickness shall depart!

It shall sweeten and make whole
Fevered breath and festered soul;
It shall mightily restrain
Over-busy hand and brain;
It shall ease thy mortal strife
'Gainst the immortal woe of life,
Till thyself restored shall prove
By what grace the Heavens do move.

Take of English flowers these—
Spring's full-faced primroses,
Summer's wild wide-hearted rose,
Autumn's wall-flower of the close,
And, thy darkness to illume,
Winter's bee-thronged ivy-bloom.

Seek and serve them where they bide
From Candlemas to Christmas-tide,
  For these simples, used aright,
  Can restore a failing sight.

These shall cleanse and purify
Webbed and inward-turning eye;
These shall show thee treasure hid,
Thy familiar fields amid;
And reveal (which is thy need)
Every man a King indeed!

THE PRAIRIE

'I SEE the grass shake in the sun for leagues on either
   hand,
   I see a river loop and run about a treeless land—
An empty plain, a steely pond, a distance diamond-clear,
And low blue naked hills beyond.   And what is that to
   fear?'

Go softly by that river-side or, when you would depart,
You'll find its every winding tied and knotted round
   your heart.
Be wary as the seasons pass, or you may ne'er outrun
The wind that sets that yellowed grass a-shiver 'neath
   the Sun.'

I hear the summer storm outblown—the drip of the
   grateful wheat.
I hear the hard trail telephone a far-off horse's feet.
I hear the horns of Autumn blow to the wildfowl overhead;
And I hear the hush before the snow.   And what is that
   to dread?'

Take heed what spell the lightning weaves—what
   charm the echoes shape—
Or, bound among a million sheaves, your soul may not
   escape.

Bar home the door of summer nights lest those hig
    planets drown
The memory of near delights in all the longed-for town

'What need have I to long or fear?   Now, friendly,
    behold
My faithful seasons robe the year in silver and in gol
Now I possess and am possessed of the land where
    would be,
And the curve of half Earth's generous breast sha
    soothe and ravish me!'

CHAPTER HEADINGS

Plain Tales from the Hills

LOOK, you have cast out Love!   What Gods are these
        You bid me please?
    The Three in One, the One in Three?   Not so!
        To my own Gods I go.
It may be they shall give me greater ease
Than your cold Christ and tangled Trinities.

'Lispeth.'

When the Earth was sick and the Skies were gray,
    And the woods were rotted with rain,
The Dead Man rode through the autumn day
    To visit his love again.

His love she neither saw nor heard,
    So heavy was her shame;
And tho' the babe within her stirred
    She knew not that he came.

'The Other Man.'

Cry 'Murder' in the market-place and each
Will turn upon his neighbour anxious eyes
That ask—'Art thou the man?'   We hunted Cain

Some centuries ago across the world.
This bred the fear our own misdeeds maintain
To-day.

'His Wedded Wife.'

Go, stalk the red deer o'er the heather,
   Ride, follow the fox if you can!
But, for pleasure and profit together,
   Allow me the hunting of Man—
The chase of the Human, the search for the Soul
   To its ruin—the hunting of Man.

'Pig.'

'Stopped in the straight when the race was his own!
Look at him cutting it—cur to the bone!'
'Ask ere the youngster be rated and chidden
What did he carry and how was he ridden?
Maybe they used him too much at the start;
Maybe Fate's weight-cloths are breaking his heart.'

'In the Pride of his Youth.'

And some are sulky, while some will plunge.
   [So ho! Steady! Stand still, you!]
Some you must gentle, and some you must lunge,
   [There! There! Who wants to kill you?]
Some—there are losses in every trade—
Will break their hearts ere bitted and made,
Will fight like fiends as the rope cuts hard,
And die dumb-mad in the breaking-yard.

'Thrown Away.'

The World hath set its heavy yoke
Upon the old white-bearded folk
Who strive to please the King.

CHAPTER HEADINGS

God's mercy is upon the young,
God's wisdom in the baby tongue
That fears not anything.
                        'Tods' Amendment.'

Not though you die to-night, O Sweet, and wail,
  A spectre at my door,
Shall mortal Fear make Love immortal fail—
  I shall but love you more,
Who, from Death's House returning, give me still
One moment's comfort in my matchless ill.
                        'By Word of Mouth.'

They burnt a corpse upon the sand—
The light shone out afar;
It guided home the plunging boats
That beat from Zanzibar.
Spirit of Fire, where'er Thy altars rise,
Thou art the Light of Guidance to our eyes!
                        'In Error.'

Ride with an idle whip, ride with an unused heel,
But, once in a way, there will come a day
When the colt must be taught to feel
The lash that falls, and the curb that galls, and the sting
  of the rowelled steel.
                'The Conversion of Aurelian McGoggin.'

It was not in the open fight
  We threw away the sword,
But in the lonely watching
  In the darkness by the ford,

37

The waters lapped, the night-wind blew,
Full-armed the Fear was born and grew,
From panic in the night.
'The Rout of the White Hussars.'

In the daytime, when she moved about me,
In the night, when she was sleeping at my side,—
I was wearied, I was wearied of her presence,
Day by day and night by night I grew to hate her—
Would God that she or I had died!
'The Bronckhorst Divorce Case.'

A stone's throw out on either hand
From that well-ordered road we tread,
And all the world is wild and strange:
Churel and ghoul and Djinn and sprite
Shall bear us company to-night,
For we have reached the Oldest Land
Wherein the Powers of Darkness range.
'In the House of Suddhoo.'

To-night, God knows what thing shall tide,
The Earth is racked and fain—
Expectant, sleepless, open-eyed;
And we, who from the Earth were made,
Thrill with our Mother's pain.
'False Dawn.'

Pit where the buffalo cooled his hide,
By the hot sun emptied, and blistered and dried;
Log in the reh-grass, hidden and lone;
Bund where the earth-rat's mounds are strown;
Cave in the bank where the sly stream steals;

Aloe that stabs at the belly and heels,
Jump if you dare on a steed untried—
Safer it is to go wide—go wide!
Hark, from in front where the best men ride:—
'Pull to the off, boys! Wide! Go wide!'

'Cupid's Arrows.'

He drank strong waters and his speech was coarse;
   He purchased raiment and forbore to pay;
He stuck a trusting junior with a horse,
   And won gymkhanas in a doubtful way.
Then, 'twixt a vice and folly, turned aside
To do good deeds and straight to cloak them, lied.

'A Bank Fraud.'

COLD IRON

'GOLD is for the mistress—silver for the maid—
  Copper for the craftsman cunning at his trade.'
'Good!' said the Baron, sitting in his hall,
'But Iron—Cold Iron—is master of them all.'

So he made rebellion 'gainst the King his liege,
Camped before his citadel and summoned it to siege.
'Nay!' said the cannoneer on the castle wall,
'But Iron—Cold Iron—shall be master of you all!'

Woe for the Baron and his knights so strong,
When the cruel cannon-balls laid 'em all along!
He was taken prisoner, he was cast in thrall,
And Iron—Cold Iron—was master of it all.

Yet his King spake kindly (ah, how kind a Lord!)
'What if I release thee now and give thee back thy
    sword?'
'Nay!' said the Baron, 'mock not at my fall,
For Iron—Cold Iron—is master of men all.'

'Tears are for the craven, prayers are for the clown—
Halters for the silly neck that cannot keep a crown.'
'As my loss is grievous, so my hope is small,
For Iron—Cold Iron—must be master of men all!'

COLD IRON

Yet his King made answer (few such Kings there be!)
'Here is Bread and here is Wine—sit and sup with me.
Eat and drink in Mary's Name, the whiles I do recall
How Iron—Cold Iron—can be master of men all!'

He took the Wine and blessed It. He blessed and
    brake the Bread.
With His own Hands He served Them, and presently
    He said:
'See! These Hands they pierced with nails, outside
    My city wall,
Show Iron—Cold Iron—to be master of men all!

'Wounds are for the desperate, blows are for the strong,
Balm and oil for weary hearts all cut and bruised with
    wrong.
I forgive thy treason—I redeem thy fall—
For Iron—Cold Iron—must be master of men all!'

'Crowns are for the valiant—sceptres for the bold!
Thrones and powers for mighty men who dare to take
    and hold.'
'Nay!' said the Baron, kneeling in his hall,
'But Iron—Cold Iron—is master of man all!
Iron out of Calvary is master of men all!'

GROWS COLD HION

Yet his King made answer (few such Kings there be!)
'Here is Bread and here is Wine, sit and sup with me.
Eat and drink in Mary's Name, the while I do recall
Who from Cold Iron—cut the master of men all!'

He took the Wine and blessed it . . . . and
brake the Bread
With His own Hands:
He said:

My city walls . . . .
Show from . . . . Cold

Wounds are for . . . .
Balm and oil for . . . .
wrong

I forgive thy tree . . . .
For from . . . . Cold Iron—must he . . . .

Crowns are for the valiant . . . .
Thrones and power and . . . .
and hold!

Nay! and the nails . . . .
But from . . . . Cold Iron—as roast . . . .
Iron out of Calvary is master of men all!'

MORNING SONG IN THE JUNGLE

ONE moment past our bodies cast
　　No shadow on the plain;
　Now clear and black they stride our track,
　　And we run home again.
In morning hush, each rock and bush
　Stands hard, and high, and raw:
Then give the Call: 'Good rest to all
　That keep the Jungle Law!'

Now horn and pelt our peoples melt
　In covert to abide;
Now, crouched and still, to cave and hill
　Our Jungle Barons glide.
Now, stark and plain, Man's oxen strain,
　That draw the new-yoked plough;
Now, stripped and dread, the dawn is red
　Above the lit talao.

Ho!　Get to lair!　The sun's aflare
　Behind the breathing grass:
And creaking through the young bamboo
　The warning whispers pass.
By day made strange, the woods we range
　With blinking eyes we scan;
While down the skies the wild duck cries:
　'The Day—the Day to Man!'

MORNING SONG IN THE JUNGLE

The dew is dried that drenched our hide,
   Or washed about our way;
And where we drank, the puddled bank
   Is crisping into clay.
The traitor Dark gives up each mark
   Of stretched or hooded claw;
Then hear the Call: 'Good rest to all
   That keep the Jungle Law!'

A CAROL

OUR Lord Who did the Ox command
　　To kneel to Judah's King,
He binds His frost upon the land
　　To ripen it for Spring—
To ripen it for Spring, good sirs,
　According to His Word.
Which well must be as ye can see—
　And who shall judge the Lord?

When we poor fenmen skate the ice
　Or shiver on the wold,
We hear the cry of a single tree
　That breaks her heart in the cold—
That breaks her heart in the cold, good sirs,
　And rendeth by the board.
Which well must be as ye can see—
　And who shall judge the Lord?

Her wood is crazed and little worth
　Excepting as to burn,
That we may warm and make our mirth
　Until the Spring return—
Until the Spring return, good sirs,
　When people walk abroad.
Which well must be as ye can see—
　And who shall judge the Lord?

A CAROL

God bless the master of this house,
  And all who sleep therein!
And guard the fens from pirate folk,
  And keep us all from sin,
To walk in honesty, good sirs,
  Of thought and deed and word!
Which shall befriend our latter end—
  And who shall judge the Lord?

'MY NEW-CUT ASHLAR'

My new-cut ashlar takes the light
    Where crimson-blank the windows flare.
By my own work before the night,
    Great Overseer, I make my prayer.

If there be good in that I wrought,
    Thy Hand compelled it, Master, Thine—
Where I have failed to meet Thy Thought
    I know, through Thee, the blame was mine.

One instant's toil to Thee denied
    Stands all Eternity's offence.
Of that I did with Thee to guide
    To Thee, through Thee, be excellence.

The depth and dream of my desire,
    The bitter paths wherein I stray—
Thou knowest Who hast made the Fire,
    Thou knowest Who hast made the Clay.

Who, lest all thought of Eden fade,
    Bring'st Eden to the craftsman's brain—
Godlike to muse o'er his own Trade
    And manlike stand with God again!

'MY NEW–CUT ASHLAR'

One stone the more swings into place
   In that dread Temple of Thy worth.
It is enough that, through Thy Grace,
   I saw nought common on Thy Earth.

Take not that vision from my ken—
   Oh whatsoe'er may spoil or speed.
Help me to need no aid from men
   That I may help such men as need!

EDDI'S SERVICE

(A.D. 687)

EDDI, priest of St. Wilfrid
　　In the chapel at Manhood End,
　Ordered a midnight service
　　For such as cared to attend.

But the Saxons were keeping Christmas,
　And the night was stormy as well.
Nobody came to service
　Though Eddi rang the bell.

'Wicked weather for walking,'
　Said Eddi of Manhood End.
'But I must go on with the service
　For such as care to attend.'

The altar-candles were lighted,—
　An old marsh donkey came,
Bold as a guest invited,
　And stared at the guttering flame.

The storm beat on at the windows,
　The water splashed on the floor,
And a wet yoke-weary bullock
　Pushed in through the open door.

'How do I know what is greatest,
  How do I know what is least?
That is My Father's business,'
  Said Eddi, Wilfrid's priest.

'But—three are gathered together—
  Listen to me and attend.
I bring good news, my brethren!'
  Said Eddi of Manhood End.

And he told the Ox of a Manger
  And a Stall in Bethlehem,
And he spoke to the Ass of a Rider,
  That rode to Jerusalem.

They steamed and dripped in the chancel,
  They listened and never stirred,
While, just as though they were Bishops,
  Eddi preached them The Word.

Till the gale blew off on the marshes
  And the windows showed the day,
And the Ox and the Ass together
  Wheeled and clattered away.

And when the Saxons mocked him,
  Said Eddi of Manhood End,
'I dare not shut His chapel
  On such as care to attend.'

SHIV AND THE GRASSHOPPER

SHIV, who poured the harvest and made the winds
    to blow,
    Sitting at the doorways of a day of long ago,
Gave to each his portion, food and toil and fate,
From the King upon the guddee to the Beggar at the
    gate.
    All things made he—Shiva the Preserver.
    Mahadeo! Mahadeo! He made all,—
    Thorn for the camel, fodder for the kine,
    And mother's heart for sleepy head, O little son of
    mine!

Wheat he gave to rich folk, millet to the poor,
Broken scraps for holy men that beg from door to door;
Cattle to the tiger, carrion to the kite,
And rags and bones to wicked wolves without the wall
    at night.
Naught he found too lofty, none he saw too low—
Parbati beside him watched them come and go;
Thought to cheat her husband, turning Shiv to jest—
Stole the little grasshopper and hid it in her breast.
    So she tricked him, Shiva the Preserver.
    Mahadeo! Mahadeo! turn and see!
    Tall are the camels, heavy are the kine,
    But this was Least of Little Things, O little son of
    mine!

SHIV AND THE GRASSHOPPER

When the dole was ended, laughingly she said,
'Master, of a million mouths is not one unfed?'
Laughing, Shiv made answer, 'All have had their part,
Even he, the little one, hidden next thy heart.'
From her breast she plucked it, Parbati the thief,
Saw the Least of Little Things gnawed a new-grown
    leaf!
Saw and feared and wondered, making prayer to Shiv,
Who hath surely given meat to all that live.

    All things made he—Shiva the Preserver.
    Mahadeo! Mahadeo! He made all,—
    Thorn for the camel, fodder for the kine,
    And mother's heart for sleepy head, O little son of
        mine!

THE FAIRIES' SIEGE

I HAVE been given my charge to keep—
    Well have I kept the same!
Playing with strife for the most of my life,
    But this is a different game.
I'll not fight against swords unseen,
    Or spears that I cannot view—
Hand him the keys of the place on your knees—
    'Tis the Dreamer whose dreams come true!

Ask for his terms and accept them at once,
    Quick, ere we anger him, go!
Never before have I flinched from the guns,
    But this is a different show.
I'll not fight with the Herald of God
    (I know what his Master can do!)
Open the gate, he must enter in state,
    'Tis the Dreamer whose dreams come true!

I'd not give way for an Emperor,
    I'd hold my road for a King—
To the Triple Crown I would not bow down—
    But this is a different thing.
I'll not fight with the Powers of Air,
    Sentry, pass him through!
Drawbridge let fall, it's the Lord of us all,
    The Dreamer whose dreams come true!

A SONG TO MITHRAS

(Hymn of the 30th Legion: circa A. D. 350)

MITHRAS, God of the Morning, our trumpets
waken the Wall!
'Rome is above the Nations, but Thou art over all!'
Now as the names are answered, and the guards are
marched away,
Mithras, also a soldier, give us strength for the day!

Mithras, God of the Noontide, the heather swims in the
heat.
Our helmets scorch our foreheads, our sandals burn our
feet.
Now in the ungirt hour—now ere we blink and drowse,
Mithras, also a soldier, keep us true to our vows!

Mithras, God of the Sunset, low on the Western main—
Thou descending immortal, immortal to rise again!
Now when the watch is ended, now when the wine is drawn!
Mithras, also a soldier, keep us pure till the dawn!

Mithras, God of the Midnight, here where the great
bull dies,
Look on thy children in darkness. Oh take our sacrifice!
Many roads thou hast fashioned—all of them lead to
the Light:
Mithras, also a soldier, teach us to die aright!

53

THE NEW KNIGHTHOOD

WHO gives him the Bath?
   'I,' said the wet,
   Rank Jungle-sweat,
'I'll give him the Bath!'

Who'll sing the psalms?
   'We,' said the Palms.
   'Ere the hot wind becalms,
We'll sing the psalms.'

Who lays on the sword?
   'I,' said the Sun,
   'Before he has done,
I'll lay on the sword.'

Who fastens his belt?
   'I,' said Short-Rations,
   'I know all the fashions
Of tightening a belt!'

Who gives him his spur?
   'I,' said his Chief,
   Exacting and brief,
'I'll give him the spur.'

THE NEW KNIGHTHOOD

Who'll shake his hand?
  'I,' said the Fever,
  'And I'm no deceiver,
I'll shake his hand.'

Who brings him the wine?
  'I,' said Quinine,
  'It's a habit of mine.
I'll come with the wine.'

Who'll put him to proof?
  'I,' said All Earth,
  'Whatever he's worth,
I'll put to the proof.'

Who'll choose him for Knight?
  'I,' said his Mother,
  'Before any other,
My very own Knight.'

And after this fashion, adventure to seek,
Was Sir Galahad made—as it might be last week!

HARP SONG OF THE DANE WOMEN

WHAT is a woman that you forsake her,
And the hearth-fire and the home-acre,
To go with the old gray Widow-maker?

She has no house to lay a guest in—
But one chill bed for all to rest in,
That the pale suns and the stray bergs nest in.

She has no strong white arms to fold you,
But the ten-times-fingering weed to hold you—
Out on the rocks where the tide has rolled you.

Yet, when the signs of summer thicken,
And the ice breaks, and the birch-buds quicken,
Yearly you turn from our side, and sicken—

Sicken again for the shouts and the slaughters.
You steal away to the lapping waters,
And look at your ship in her winter quarters.

You forget our mirth, and talk at the tables,
The kine in the shed and the horse in the stables—
To pitch her sides and go over her cables.

56

HARP SONG OF THE DANE WOMEN

Then you drive out where the storm-clouds swallow,
And the sound of your oar-blades, falling hollow,
Is all we have left through the months to follow.

Ah, what is Woman that you forsake her,
And the hearth-fire and the home-acre,
To go with the old gray Widow-maker?

Then you drive out where the storm-clouds swallow,

THE THOUSANDTH MAN

ONE man in a thousand, Solomon says,
  Will stick more close than a brother.
And it's worth while seeking him half your days
  If you find him before the other.
Nine hundred and ninety-nine depend
  On what the world sees in you,
But the Thousandth Man will stand your friend
  With the whole round world agin you.

'Tis neither promise nor prayer nor show
  Will settle the finding for 'ee.
Nine hundred and ninety-nine of 'em go
  By your looks or your acts or your glory.
But if he finds you and you find him,
  The rest of the world don't matter;
For the Thousandth Man will sink or swim
  With you in any water.

You can use his purse with no more talk
  Than he uses yours for his spendings,
And laugh and meet in your daily walk
  As though there had been no lendings.
Nine hundred and ninety-nine of 'em call
  For silver and gold in their dealings;
But the Thousandth Man he's worth 'em all,
  Because you can show him your feelings.

THE THOUSANDTH MAN

His wrong's your wrong, and his right's your right,
   In season or out of season.
Stand up and back it in all men's sight—
   With that for your only reason!
Nine hundred and ninety-nine can't bide
   The shame or mocking or laughter,
But the Thousandth Man will stand by your side
   To the gallows-foot—and after!

THE WINNERS

WHAT is the moral?   Who rides may read.
  When the night is thick and the tracks are blind
A friend at a pinch is a friend indeed,
  But a fool to wait for the laggard behind.
Down to Gehenna or up to the Throne,
He travels the fastest who travels alone.

White hands cling to the tightened rein,
  Slipping the spur from the booted heel,
Tenderest voices cry 'Turn again,'
  Red lips tarnish the scabbarded steel,
High hopes faint on a warm hearth-stone—
He travels the fastest who travels alone.

One may fall but he falls by himself—
  Falls by himself with himself to blame,
One may attain and to him is pelf,
  Loot of the city in Gold or Fame.
Plunder of earth shall be all his own
Who travels the fastest and travels alone.

Wherefore the more ye be holpen and stayed
  Stayed by a friend in the hour of toil,
Sing the heretical song I have made—
  His be the labour and yours be the spoil.
Win by his aid and the aid disown—
He travels the fastest who travels alone.

'BROWN BESS'

IN the days of lace-ruffles, perukes, and brocade,
    Brown Bess was a partner whom none could de-
        spise—
An outspoken, flinty-lipped, brazen-faced jade,
    With a habit of looking men straight in the eyes.
At Blenheim and Ramillies fops would confess
They were pierced to the heart by the charms of Brown
    Bess.

Though her sight was not long and her weight was not
    small,
    Yet her actions were winning, her language was clear;
And every one bowed as she opened the ball
    On the arm of some high-gaitered, grim grenadier.
Half Europe admitted the striking success
Of the dances and routs that were given by Brown Bess.

When ruffles were turned into stiff leather stocks
    And people wore pigtails instead of perukes,
Brown Bess never altered her iron-gray locks,
    She knew she was valued for more than her looks.
'Oh, powder and patches was always my dress,
And I think I am killing enough,' said Brown Bess.

So she followed her red-coats, whatever they did,
    From the heights of Quebec to the plains of Assaye,
From Gibraltar to Acre, Cape Town and Madrid,

And nothing about her was changed on the way;
(But most of the Empire which now we possess
Was won through those years by old-fashioned **Brown
    Bess**.)

In stubborn retreat or in stately advance,
    From the Portugal coast to the cork-woods of Spain,
She had puzzled some excellent Marshals of France
    Till none of them wanted to meet her again:
But later, near Brussels, Napoleon—no less—
Arranged for a Waterloo ball with Brown Bess.

She had danced till the dawn of that terrible day—
    She danced on till dusk of more terrible night,
And before her linked squares his battalions gave way,
    And her long fierce quadrilles put his lancers to flight.
And when his gilt carriage drove off in the press,
'I have danced my last dance for the world!' said Brown
    Bess.

If you go to Museums—there's one in Whitehall—
    Where old weapons are shown with their names writ
    beneath,
You will find her, upstanding, her back to the wall,
    As stiff as a ramrod, the flint in her teeth.
And if ever we English have reason to bless
Any arm save our mothers', that arm is Brown Bess!

'How far is St. Helena from the Beresina ice?'

How far is St. Helena from the field of Waterloo?

A ST. HELENA LULLABY

'HOW far is St. Helena from a little child at play?'
    What makes you want to wander there with
        all the world between?
Oh, Mother, call your son again or else he'll run away.
    (No one thinks of winter when the grass is green!)

'How far is St. Helena from a fight in Paris street?'
    I haven't time to answer now—the men are falling
        fast.
The guns begin to thunder, and the drums begin to beat.
    (If you take the first step you will take the last!)

'How far is St. Helena from the field of Austerlitz?'
    You couldn't hear me if I told—so loud the cannons
        roar.
But not so far for people who are living by their wits.
    ('Gay go up' means 'Gay go down' the wide world
        o'er!)

'How far is St. Helena from an Emperor of France?'
    I cannot see—I cannot tell—the crowns they dazzle
        so.
The Kings sit down to dinner, and the Queens stand up
        to dance.
    (After open weather you may look for snow!)

63

'How far is St. Helena from the Capes of Trafalgar?'
  A longish way—a longish way—with ten year more
    to run.
It's South across the water underneath a setting star.
  (What you cannot finish you must leave undone!)

'How far is St. Helena from the Beresina ice?'
  An ill way—a chill way—the ice begins to crack.
But not so far for gentlemen who never took advice.
  (When you can't go forward you must e'en come back!)

'How far is St. Helena from the field of Waterloo?'
  A near way—a clear way—the ship will take you soon.
A pleasant place for gentlemen with little left to do.
  (Morning never tries you till the afternoon!)

'How far from St. Helena to the Gate of Heaven's
    Grace?'
  That no one knows—that no one knows—and no one
    ever will.
But fold your hands across your heart and cover up
    your face,
  And after all your trapesings, child, lie still.

CHIL'S SONG

fed!

CHIL'S SONG

THESE were my companions going forth by night—
(For Chil! Look you, for Chil!)
Now come I to whistle them the ending of the
fight.
(Chil! Vanguards of Chil!)
Word they gave me overhead of quarry newly slain,
Word I gave them underfoot of buck upon the plain.
Here's an end of every trail—they shall not speak again!

They that called the hunting-cry—they that followed
fast—
(For Chil! Look you, for Chil!)
They that bade the sambhur wheel, or pinned him as he
passed—
(Chil! Vanguards of Chil!)
They that lagged behind the scent—they that ran be-
fore,
They that shunned the level horn—they that overbore.
Here's an end of every trail—they shall not follow more.

These were my companions. Pity 'twas they died!
(For Chil! Look you, for Chil!)
Now come I to comfort them that knew them in their
pride.
(Chil! Vanguards of Chil!)

CHIL'S SONG

Tattered flank and sunken eye, open mouth and red,
Locked and lank and lone they lie, the dead upon their
dead.
Here's an end of every trail—and here my hosts are
fed!

THE CAPTIVE

NOT with an outcry to Allah nor any complaining
    He answered his name at the muster and stood
    to the chaining.
When the twin anklets were nipped on the leg-bars that
    held them,
He brotherly greeted the armourers stooping to weld
    them.
Ere the sad dust of the marshalled feet of the chain-gang
    swallowed him
Observing him nobly at ease, I alighted and followed
    him.
Thus we had speech by the way, but not touching his
    sorrow—
Rather his red Yesterday and his regal To-morrow,
Wherein he statelily moved to the click of his chains
    unregarded,
Nowise abashed but contented to drink of the potion
    awarded.
Saluting aloofly his Fate, he made swift with his story,
And the words of his mouth were as slaves spreading
    carpets of glory
Embroidered with names of the Djinns—a miraculous
    weaving—
But the cool and perspicuous eye overbore unbeliev-
    ing.

So I submitted myself to the limits of rapture—
Bound by this man we had bound, amid captives his
    capture—
Till he returned me to earth and the visions departed.
But on him be the Peace and the Blessing; for he was
    great-hearted!

THE PUZZLER

THE Celt in all his variants from Builth to Bally-
    hoo,
    His mental processes are plain—one knows what
    he will do,
And can logically predicate his finish by his start;
But the English—ah, the English—they are quite a race
    apart.

Their psychology is bovine, their outlook crude and raw.
They abandon vital matters to be tickled with a straw,
But the straw that they were tickled with—the chaff
    that they were fed with—
They convert into a weaver's beam to break their foe-
    man's head with.

For undemocratic reasons and for motives not of State,
They arrive at their conclusions—largely inarticulate.
Being void of self-expression they confide their views to
    none;
But sometimes in a smoking-room, one learns why
    things were done.

Yes, sometimes in a smoking-room, through clouds of
    'Ers' and 'Ums'
Obliquely and by inference illumination comes,

On some step that they have taken, or some action they
    approve—
Embellished with the argot of the Upper Fourth Re-
    move.

In telegraphic sentences, half nodded to their friends,
They hint a matter's inwardness—and there the matter
    ends.
And while the Celt is talking from Valencia to Kirkwall,
The English—ah, the English!—don't say anything at
    all!

THE REEDS OF RUNNYMEDE

At Runnymede, at Runnymede,
  What say the reeds at Runnymede?
  The lissom reeds that give and take,
That bend so far, but never break,
They keep the sleepy Thames awake
  With tales of John at Runnymede.

At Runnymede, at Runnymede,
  Oh hear the reeds at Runnymede!
'You mustn't sell, delay, deny,
A freeman's right or liberty,
It wakes the stubborn Englishry,
  We saw 'em roused at Runnymede!

'When through our ranks the Barons came,
With little thought of praise or blame,
But resolute to play the game,
  They lumbered up to Runnymede;
And there they launched in solid line,
The first attack on Right Divine—
The curt, uncompromising "Sign!"
  That settled John at Runnymede.

'At Runnymede, at Runnymede,
Your rights were won at Runnymede!
No freeman shall be fined or bound,
  Or dispossessed of freehold ground,

71

THE REEDS OF RUNNYMEDE

Except by lawful judgment found
And passed upon him by his peers!—
Forget not, after all these years,
  The charter signed at Runnymede.'

And still when mob or monarch lays
Too rude a hand on English ways,
The whisper wakes, the shudder plays,
  Across the reeds at Runnymede.
And Thames, that knows the moods of kings,
And crowds and priests and suchlike things,
Rolls deep and dreadful as he brings
  Their warning down from Runnymede!

HADRAMAUTI

WHO knows the heart of the Christian?   How does he reason?
  What are his measures and balances?   Which is his season
For laughter, forbearance or bloodshed, and what devils move him
When he arises to smite us?   I do not love him.

He invites the derision of strangers—he enters all places.
Booted, bareheaded he enters.   With shouts and embraces
He asks of us news of the household whom we reckon nameless.
Certainly Allah created him forty-fold shameless.

So it is not in the Desert.   One came to me weeping—
The Avenger of Blood on his track—I took him in keeping,
Demanding not whom he had slain, I refreshed him, I fed him
As he were even a brother.   But Eblis had bred him.

He was the son of an ape, ill at ease in his clothing,
He talked with his head, hands and feet.   I endured him with loathing.
Whatever his spirit conceived his countenance showed it
As a frog shows in a mud-puddle.   Yet I abode it!

I fingered my beard and was dumb, in silence confronting him.

His soul was too shallow for silence, e'en with Death hunting him.

I said: ' 'Tis his weariness speaks,' but, when he had rested,

He chirped in my face like some sparrow, and, presently, jested!

Wherefore slew I that stranger? He brought me dishonour.

I saddled my mare, Bijli, I set him upon her.

I gave him rice and goat's flesh. He bared me to laughter.

When he was gone from my tent, swift I followed after,

Taking my sword in my hand. The hot wine had filled him.

Under the stars he mocked me—therefore I killed him!

GALLIO'S SONG

(And Gallio cared for none of these things.—
Acts xviii. 17)

ALL day long to the judgment-seat
    The crazed Provincials drew—
All day long at their ruler's feet
    Howled for the blood of the Jew.
Insurrection with one accord
    Banded itself and woke,
And Paul was about to open his mouth
    When Achaia's Deputy spoke—

'Whether the God descend from above
    Or the Man ascend upon high,
Whether this maker of tents be Jove
    Or a younger deity—
I will be no judge between your gods
    And your godless bickerings.
Lictor, drive them hence with rods.
    I care for none of these things!

'Were it a question of lawful due
    Or Cæsar's rule denied,
Reason would I should bear with you
    And order it well to be tried;

But this is a question of words and names.
  I know the strife it brings.
I will not pass upon any your claims.
  I care for none of these things.

'One thing only I see most clear,
  As I pray you also see.
Claudius Cæsar hath set me here
  Rome's Deputy to be.
It is Her peace that ye go to break—
  Not mine, nor any king's,
But, touching your clamour of "Conscience sake,"
  I care for none of these things.

'Whether ye rise for the sake of a creed,
  Or riot in hope of spoil,
Equally will I punish the deed,
  Equally check the broil;
Nowise permitting injustice at all
  From whatever doctrine it springs—
But—whether ye follow Priapus or Paul,
  I care for none of these things.'

THE BEES AND THE FLIES

A FARMER of the Augustan Age
  Perused in Virgil's golden page,
  The story of the secret won
From Proteus by Cyrene's son—
How the dank sea-god showed the swain
Means to restore his hives again.
More briefly, how a slaughtered bull
Breeds honey by the bellyful.

The egregious rustic put to death
A bull by stopping of its breath,
Disposed the carcass in a shed
With fragrant herbs and branches spread,
And, having thus performed the charm,
Sat down to wait the promised swarm.

Nor waited long.   The God of Day
Impartial, quickening with his ray
Evil and good alike, beheld
The carcass—and the carcass swelled.
Big with new birth the belly heaves
Beneath its screen of scented leaves,
Past any doubt, the bull conceives!

The farmer bids men bring more hives
To house the profit that arrives;

77

Prepares on pan, and key and kettle,
Sweet music that shall make 'em settle;
But when to crown the work he goes,
Gods! What a stink salutes his nose!
Where are the honest toilers?   Where
The gravid mistress of their care?
A busy scene, indeed, he sees,
But not a sign or sound of bees.
Worms of the riper grave unhid
By any kindly coffin lid,
Obscene and shameless to the light
Seethe in insatiate appetite,
Through putrid offal, while above
The hissing blow-fly seeks his love,
Whose offspring, supping where they supt,
Consume corruption twice corrupt.

Brother, thy tail hangs down behind!
       things!

ROAD–SONG OF THE BANDAR–LOG

HERE we go in a flung festoon,
    Half-way up to the jealous moon!
    Don't you envy our pranceful bands?
Don't you wish you had extra hands?
Wouldn't you like if your tails were—so—
Curved in the shape of a Cupid's bow?
        Now you're angry, but—never mind,
        Brother, thy tail hangs down behind!

Here we sit in a branchy row,
Thinking of beautiful things we know;
Dreaming of deeds that we mean to do,
All complete, in a minute or two—
Something noble and grand and good,
Won by merely wishing we could.
        Now we're going to—never mind,
        Brother, thy tail hangs down behind!

All the talk we ever have heard
Uttered by bat or beast or bird—
Hide or fin or scale or feather—
Jabber it quickly and all together!
Excellent! Wonderful! Once again!
Now we are talking just like men.

79

Let's pretend we are . . . never mind,
Brother, thy tail hangs down behind!
This is the way of the Monkey-kind!

Then join our leaping lines that scumfish through the
     pines,
That rocket by where, light and high, the wild-grape
     swings.
By the rubbish in our wake, and the noble noise we
     make,
Be sure, be sure, we're going to do some splendid things!

'OUR FATHERS ALSO'

THRONES, Powers, Dominions, Peoples, Kings,
    Are changing 'neath our hand;
    Our fathers also see these things,
    But they do not understand.

By—they are by with mirth and tears,
    Wit or the works of Desire—
Cushioned about on the kindly years
    Between the wall and the fire.

The grapes are pressed, the corn is shocked—
    Standeth no more to glean;
For the Gates of Love and Learning locked
    When they went out between.

All lore our Lady Venus bares,
    Signalled it was or told
By the dear lips long given to theirs
    And longer to the mould.

All Profit, all Device, all Truth
    Written it was or said
By the mighty men of their mighty youth,
    Which is mighty being dead.

'OUR FATHERS ALSO'

The film that floats before their eyes
   The Temple's Veil they call;
And the dust that on the Shewbread lies
   Is holy over all.

Warn them of seas that slip our yoke
   Of slow-conspiring stars—
The ancient Front of Things unbroke
   But heavy with new wars?

By—they are by with mirth and tears,
   Wit or the waste of Desire—
Cushioned about on the kindly years
   Between the wall and the fire.

CHAPTER HEADINGS

The Naulahka

WE meet in an evil land
    That is near to the gates of hell.
  I wait for thy command
To serve, to speed or withstand.
And thou sayest, I do not well?

Oh Love, the flowers so red
  Are only tongues of flame,
The earth is full of the dead,
The new-killed, restless dead.
There is danger beneath and o'erhead;
    And I guard thy gates in fear
      Of peril and jeopardy,
    Of words thou canst not hear,
      Of signs thou canst not see—
And thou sayest 'tis ill that I come?

This I saw when the rites were done,
And the lamps were dead and the Gods alone,
And the gray snake coiled on the altar stone.
  Ere I fled from a Fear that I could not see,
  And the Gods of the East made mouths at me.

Now, it is not good for the Christian's health to hustle
    the Aryan brown,
For the Christian riles, and the Aryan smiles, and he
    weareth the Christian down;
And the end of the fight is a tombstone white, with the
    name of the late deceased,
And the epitaph drear: 'A fool lies here who tried to
    hustle the East.'

    Beat off in our last fight were we?
    The greater need to seek the sea.
    For Fortune changeth as the moon
    To caravel and picaroon.
    Then Eastward Ho! Or Westward Ho!
    Whichever wind may meetest blow.
    Our quarry sails on either sea,
    Fat prey for such bold lads as we.
    And every sun-dried buccaneer
    Must hand and reef and watch and steer,
    And bear great wrath of sea and sky
    Before the plate-ships wallow by.
    Now as our tall bows take the foam,
    Let no man turn his heart to home,
    Save to desire treasure more
    And larger warehouse for his store,
    When treasure trove from Santos Bay
    Shall make our sea-washed village gay.

    Because I sought it far from men
    In deserts and alone;
    I found it burning overhead,
    The jewel of a Throne.

Because I sought—I sought it so
    And spent my days to find—
It blazed one moment ere it left
    The blacker night behind!

When a lover hies abroad
    Looking for his love,
Azrael smiling sheathes his sword,
    Heaven smiles above.
Earth and sea
His servants be
And to lesser compass round
That his love be sooner found.

There was a strife 'twixt man and maid—
    Oh that was at the birth of time!
But what befell 'twixt man and maid,
    Oh that's beyond the grip of rhyme.
'Twas, 'Sweet, I must not bide with you,'
    And, 'Love, I cannot bide alone';
For both were young and both were true,
    And both were hard as the nether stone.

There is pleasure in the wet wet clay,
    When the artist's hand is potting it;
There is pleasure in the wet wet lay,
    When the poet's pad is blotting it;
There is pleasure in the shine of your picture on the
    line
    At the Royal Acade-my;

But the pleasure felt in these is as chalk to Cheddar
  cheese,
   When it comes to a well-made Lie.
    To a quite unwreckable Lie,
    To a most impeccable Lie!
To a water-tight, fireproof, angle-iron, sunk-hinge, time-
  lock, steel-faced Lie!
    Not a private hansom Lie,
    But a pair-and-brougham Lie,
Not a little-place-at-Tooting, but a country-house-with-
  shooting
    And a ring-fence-deer-park Lie.

   We be the Gods of the East—
    Older than all—
   Masters of Mourning and Feast,
    How shall we fall?

  Will they gape for the husks that ye proffer,
   Or yearn to your song?
  And we—have we nothing to offer
   Who ruled them so long—
In the fume of the incense, the clash of the cymbal, the
  blare of the conch and the gong?

   Over the strife of the schools
    Low the day burns—
   Back with the kine from the pools
    Each one returns
To the life that he knows where the altar-flame glows
  and the tulsi is trimmed in the urns.

86

CHAPTER HEADINGS

The Light that Failed

So we settled it all when the storm was done
  As comfy as comfy could be;
And I was to wait in the barn, my dears,
  Because I was only three.
And Teddy would run to the rainbow's foot
  Because he was five and a man;
And that's how it all began, my dears,
  And that's how it all began.

'If I have taken the common clay
  And wrought it cunningly
In the shape of a God that was digged a clod,
  The greater honour to me.'
'If thou hast taken the common clay,
  And thy hands be not free
From the taint of the soil, thou hast made thy spoil
  The greater shame to thee.'

The wolf-cub at even lay hid in the corn,
  Where the smoke of the cooking hung gray:
He knew where the doe made a couch for her fawn,
  And he looked to his strength for his prey.
  But the moon swept the smoke-wreaths away,
And he turned from his meal in the villager's close,
And he bayed to the moon as she rose.

    The lark will make her hymn to God,
      The partridge call her brood,
    While I forget the heath I trod,
      The fields wherein I stood.

'Tis dule to know not night from morn,
But greater dule to know
I can but hear the hunter's horn
That once I used to blow.

There were three friends that buried the fourth,
The mould in his mouth and the dust in his eyes,
And they went south and east and north—
The strong man fights but the sick man dies.

There were three friends that spoke of the dead—
The strong man fights but the sick man dies—
'And would he were here with us now,' they said,
'The sun in our face and the wind in our eyes.'

Yet at the last, ere our spearmen had found him,
Yet at the last, ere a sword-thrust could save,
Yet at the last, with his masters around him,
He spoke of the Faith as a master to slave.

Yet at the last, though the Kafirs had maimed him,
Broken by bondage and wrecked by the reiver,
Yet at the last, tho' the darkness had claimed him,
He called upon Allah, and died a Believer!

A BRITISH–ROMAN SONG

(A. D. 406)

MY father's father saw it not,
    And I, belike, shall never come
  To look on that so-holy spot—
      The very Rome—

Crowned by all Time, all Art, all Might,
    The equal work of Gods and Man,
City beneath whose oldest height—
      The Race began!

Soon to send forth again a brood,
    Unshakeable, we pray, that clings,
To Rome's thrice-hammered hardihood—
      In arduous things.

Strong heart with triple armour bound,
    Beat strongly, for thy life-blood runs,
Age after Age, the Empire round—
      In us thy Sons,

Who, distant from the Seven Hills,
    Loving and serving much, require
Thee—thee to guard 'gainst home-born ills,
      The Imperial Fire!

A PICT SONG

ROME never looks where she treads.
    Always her heavy hooves fall,
    On our stomachs, our hearts or our heads;
    And Rome never heeds when we bawl.
Her sentries pass on—that is all,
    And we gather behind them in hordes,
And plot to reconquer the Wall,
    With only our tongues for our swords.

We are the Little Folk—we!
    Too little to love or to hate.
Leave us alone and you'll see
    How we can drag down the State!
We are the worm in the wood!
    We are the rot at the root!
We are the germ in the blood!
    We are the thorn in the foot!

Mistletoe killing an oak—
    Rats gnawing cables in two—
Moths making holes in a cloak—
    How they must love what they do!
Yes—and we Little Folk too,
    We are busy as they—
Working our works out of view—
    Watch, and you'll see it some day!

A PICT SONG

No indeed! We are not strong,
  But we know Peoples that are.
Yes, and we'll guide them along,
  To smash and destroy you in War!
We shall be slaves just the same?
  Yes, we have always been slaves,
But you—you will die of the shame,
  And then we shall dance on your graves!

  We are the Little Folk—we, etc.

THE PICTS' WORK

WHEN Rome was rotten-ripe to her fall,
    And the sceptre passed from her hand,
The pestilent Picts leaped over the wall
    To harry the British land.

The little dark men of the mountain and waste,
    So quick to laughter and tears,
They came panting with hate and haste
    For the loot of five hundred years.

They killed the trader, they sacked the shops,
    They ruined temple and town—
They swept like wolves through the standing crops
    Crying that Rome was down.

They wiped out all that they could find
    Of beauty and strength and worth,
But they could not wipe out the Viking's Wind,
    That brings the ships from the North.

They could not wipe out the North-East gales,
    Nor what those gales set free—
The pirate ships with their close-reefed sails,
    Leaping from sea to sea.

THE PICTS' WORK

They had forgotten the shield-hung hull
   Seen nearer and more plain,
Dipping into the troughs like a gull,
   And gull-like rising again.

The painted eyes that glare and frown,
   In the high snake-headed stem,
Searching the beach while her sail comes down,
   They had forgotten them!

There was no Count of the Saxon Shore
   To meet her hand to hand,
When she took the beach with a lunge and a roar,
   And the pirates rushed inland!

DANE–GELD

IT is always a temptation to an armed and agile nation
  To call upon a neighbour and to say:—
'We invaded you last night—we are quite prepared
    to fight,
  Unless you pay us cash to go away.'

(Waltz-time)
          And that is called asking for Dane-geld,
            And the people who ask it explain
          That you've only to pay 'em the Dane-geld
            And then you'll get rid of the Dane!

It is always a temptation to a rich and lazy nation,
  To puff and look important and to say:—
'Though we know we should defeat you, we have not the
    time to meet you,
  We will therefore pay you cash to go away.'

          And that is called paying the Dane-geld;
            But we've proved it again and again,
          That, once you have paid him the Dane-geld,
            You never get rid of the Dane.

It is wrong to put temptation in the path of any nation,
  For fear they should succumb and go astray,
So when you are requested to pay up or be molested,
  You will find it better policy to say:—

DANE–GELD

'We never pay any one Dane-geld,
  No matter how trifling the cost,
For the end of that game is oppression and shame,
  And the nation that plays it is lost!'

THE STRANGER

THE Stranger within my gate,
  He may be true or kind,
But he does not talk my talk—
  I cannot feel his mind.
I see the face and the eyes and the mouth,
  But not the soul behind.

The men of my own stock
  They may do ill or well,
But they tell the lies I am wonted to,
  They are used to the lies I tell.
We do not need interpreters
  When we go to buy and sell.

The Stranger within my gates,
  He may be evil or good,
But I cannot tell what powers control—
  What reasons sway his mood;
Nor when the Gods of his far-off land
  May repossess his blood.

The men of my own stock,
  Bitter bad they may be,
But, at least, they hear the things I hear,
  And see the things I see;
And whatever I think of them and their likes
  They think of the likes of me.

THE STRANGER

This was my father's belief
  And this is also mine:
Let the corn be all one sheaf—
  And the grapes be all one vine,
Ere our children's teeth are set on edge
  By bitter bread and wine.

'RIMINI'

(Marching Song of a Roman Legion of the Later Empire)

WHEN I left Rome for Lalage's sake
    By the Legions' road to Rimini,
She vowed her heart was mine to take
With me and my shield to Rimini
(Till the Eagles flew from Rimini.)
    And I've tramped Britain, and I've tramped Gaul,
    And the Pontic shore where the snow-flakes fall
As white as the neck of Lalage—
(As cold as the heart of Lalage!)
    And I've lost Britain, and I've lost Gaul,
    And I've lost Rome, and worst of all,
        I've lost Lalage!

When you go by the Via Aurelia,
    As thousands have travelled before,
Remember the Luck of the Soldier
    Who never saw Rome any more!
Oh dear was the sweetheart that kissed him,
    And dear was the mother that bore,
But his shield was picked up in the heather,
    And he never saw Rome any more!

    And he left Rome, etc.

98

'RIMINI'

When you go by the Via Aurelia
  That runs from the City to Gaul,
Remember the Luck of the Soldier
  Who rose to be master of all!
He carried the sword and the buckler,
  He mounted his guard on the Wall,
Till the Legions elected him Cæsar,
  And he rose to be master of all!

  And he left Rome, etc.

It's twenty-five marches to Narbo,
  It's forty-five more up the Rhone,
And the end may be death in the heather
  Or life on an Emperor's throne.
But whether the Eagles obey us,
  Or we go to the Ravens—alone,
I'd sooner be Lalage's lover
  Than sit on an Emperor's throne!

  We've all left Rome for Lalage's sake, etc.

'POOR HONEST MEN'

(A. D. 1800)

YOUR jar of Virginny
  Will cost you a guinea,
  Which you reckon too much by five shillings or
      ten;
But light your churchwarden
And judge it according,
When I've told you the troubles of poor honest men.

From the Capes of the Delaware,
As you are well aware,
We sail with tobacco for England—but then,
Our own British cruisers,
They watch us come through, sirs,
And they press half a score of us poor honest men!

Or if by quick sailing
(Thick weather prevailing)
We leave them behind (as we do now and then)
We are sure of a gun from
Each frigate we run from,
Which is often destruction to poor honest men!

Broadsides the Atlantic
We tumble short-handed,
With shot-holes to plug and new canvas to bend,

100

'POOR HONEST MEN'

And off the Azores,
Dutch, Dons and Monsieurs
Are waiting to terrify poor honest men.

Napoleon's embargo
Is laid on all cargo
Which comfort or aid to King George may intend;
And since roll, twist and leaf,
Of all comforts is chief,
They try for to steal it from poor honest men!

With no heart for fight,
We take refuge in flight,
But fire as we run, our retreat to defend,
Until our stern-chasers
Cut up her fore-braces,
And she flies up the wind from us poor honest men!

Twix' the Forties and Fifties
South-eastward the drift is,
And so, when we think we are making Land's End,
Alas, it is Ushant
With half the King's Navy,
Blockading French ports against poor honest men!

But they may not quit station
(Which is our salvation)
So swiftly we stand to the Nor'ard again;
And finding the tail of
A homeward-bound convoy,
We slip past the Scillies like poor honest men.

Twix' the Lizard and Dover
We hand our stuff over,
Though I may not inform how we do it, nor when;
But a light on each quarter
Low down on the water
Is well understanded by poor honest men!

Even then we have dangers
From meddlesome strangers
Who spy on our business and are not content
To take a smooth answer,
Except with a handspike   .   .   .
And they say they are murdered by poor honest men!

To be drowned or be shot
Is our natural lot,
Why should we, moreover, be hanged in the end—
After all our great pains
For to dangle in chains
As though we were smugglers, not poor honest men?

THE BOATS OF NEWHAVEN

THE boats of Newhaven and Folkestone and Dover
To Dieppe and Boulogne and to Calais cross over;
And in each of those runs there is not a square yard
Where theEnglish and French haven't fought and fought
  hard!

If the ships that were sunk could be floated once more,
They'd stretch like a raft from the shore to the shore,
And we'd see, as we crossed, every pattern and plan
Of ship that was built since sea-fighting began.

There'd be biremes and brigantines, cutters and sloops,
Cogs, carracks and galleons with gay gilded poops—
Hoys, caravels, ketches, corvettes and the rest,
As thick as regattas, from Ramsgate to Brest.

But the galleys of Cæsar, the squadrons of Sluys,
And Nelson's crack frigates are hid from our eyes,
Where the high Seventy-fours of Napoleon's days
Lie down with Deal luggers and French chasse-marees.

They'll answer no signal—they rest on the ooze
With their honeycombed guns and their skeleton crews—
And racing above them, through sunshine or gale,
The Cross-Channel packets come in with the Mail.

Then the poor sea-sick passengers, English and French,
Must open their trunks on the Custom-house bench,
While the officers rummage for smuggled cigars
And nobody thinks of our bloodthirsty wars!

'WHEN THE GREAT ARK'

WHEN the Great Ark, in Vigo Bay,
    Rode stately through the half-manned fleet,
    From every ship about her way
    She heard the mariners entreat—
'Before we take the seas again
Let down your boats and send us men!

'We have no lack of victual here
    With work—God knows!—enough for all,
To hand and reef and watch and steer,
    Because our present strength is small.
While your three decks are crowded so
Your crews can scarcely stand or go.

'In war, your numbers do but raise
    Confusion and divided will;
In storm, the mindless deep obeys
    Not multitudes but single skill;
In calm, your numbers, closely pressed,
Do breed a mutiny or pest.

'We, even on unchallenged seas,
    Dare not adventure where we would,
But forfeit brave advantages
    For lack of men to make 'em good;
Whereby, to England's double cost,
Honour and profit both are lost!'

105

THE SONG OF VALLEY FORGE

'TWAS not while England's sword unsheathed
    Put half a world to flight,
    Nor while their new-built cities breathed
    Secure behind her might;
Not while she poured from Pole to Line
    Treasure and ships and men—
These worshippers at Freedom's shrine
    They did not quit her then!

Not till their foes were driven forth
    By England o'er the main—
Not till the Frenchman from the North
    Had gone, with shattered Spain;
Not till the clean-swept ocean showed
    No hostile flag unrolled,
Did they remember what they owed
    To Freedom—and were bold!

The snow lies thick on Valley Forge,
    The ice on the Delaware,
But the poor dead soldiers of King George
    They neither know nor care—

Not though the earliest primrose break
    On the sunny side of the lane,
And scuffling rookeries awake
    Their England's spring again.

THE SONG OF VALLEY FORGE

They will not stir when the drifts are gone
   Or the ice melts out of the bay,
And the men that served with Washington
   Lie all as still as they.

They will not stir though the mayflower blows
   In the moist dark woods of pine,
And every rock-strewn pasture shows
   Mullein and columbine.

Each for his land, in a fair fight,
   Encountered, strove, and died,
And the kindly earth that knows no spite
   Covers them side by side.

She is too busy to think of war;
   She has all the world to make gay,
And, behold, the yearly flowers are
   Where they were in our fathers' day!

Golden-rod by the pasture wall
   When the columbine is dead,
And sumach leaves that turn, in fall,
   Bright as the blood they shed.

PROPHETS AT HOME

PROPHETS have honour all over the Earth,
    Except in the village where they were born;
Where such as knew them boys from birth,
    Nature-ally hold 'em in scorn.

When Prophets are naughty and young and vain,
    They make a won'erful grievance of it.
(You can see by their writings how they complain),
    But O, 'tis won'erful good for the Prophet!

There's nothing Nineveh Town can give
    (Nor being swallowed by whales between),
Makes up for the place where a man's folk live,
    Which don't care nothing what he has been.
He might ha' been that, or he might ha' been this,
But they love and they hate him for what he is.

THE DUTCH IN THE MEDWAY

IF war were won by feasting,
　　Or victory by song,
　Or safety found in sleeping sound,
　　How England would be strong!
But honour and dominion
　Are not maintained so,
They're only got by sword and shot,
　And this the Dutchmen know!

The moneys that should feed us,
　You spend on your delight,
How can you then have sailor-men
　To aid you in your fight?
Our fish and cheese are rotten,
　Which makes the scurvy grow—
We cannot serve you if we starve,
　And this the Dutchmen know!

Our ships in every harbour
　Be neither whole nor sound,
And, when we seek to mend a leak,
　No oakum can be found,
Or, if it is, the caulkers,
　And carpenters also,
For lack of pay have run away,
　And this the Dutchmen know!

Mere powder, guns, and bullets,
  We scarce can get at all.
Their price was spent in merriment
  And revel at Whitehall,
While we in tattered doublets
  From ship to ship must row,
Beseeching friends for odds and ends—
  And this the Dutchmen know!

No King will heed our warnings,
  No Court will pay our claims—
Our King and Court for their disport
  Do sell the very Thames!
For, now De Ruyter's topsails,
  Off naked Chatham show,
We dare not meet him with our fleet—
  And this the Dutchmen know!

JUBAL AND TUBAL CAIN

JUBAL sang of the Wrath of God
  And the curse of thistle and thorn—
But Tubal got him a pointed rod,
  And scrabbled the earth for corn.
    Old—old as that early mould,
      Young as the sprouting grain—
    Yearly green is the strife between
      Jubal and Tubal Cain!

Jubal sang of the new-found sea,
  And the love that its waves divide—
But Tubal hollowed a fallen tree
  And passed to the farther side.
    Black—black as the hurricane-wrack,
      Salt as the under-main—
    Bitter and cold is the hate they hold—
      Jubal and Tubal Cain!

Jubal sang of the golden years
  When wars and wounds shall cease—
But Tubal fashioned the hand-flung spears
  And showed his neighbours peace.
    New—new as the Nine-point-two,
      Older than Lamech's slain—
    Roaring and loud is the feud avowed
      Twix' Jubal and Tubal Cain!

Jubal sang of the cliffs that bar
　　And the peaks that none may crown—
But Tubal clambered by jut and scar
　　And there he builded a town.
　　　High—high as the snowsheds lie,
　　　　Low as the culverts drain—
　　　Wherever they be they can never agree—
　　　　Jubal and Tubal Cain!

THE VOORTREKKER

THE gull shall whistle in his wake, the blind wave
break in fire.
He shall fulfil God's utmost will, unknowing his
desire.
And he shall see old planets change and alien stars arise,
And give the gale his seaworn sail in shadow of new skies.
Strong lust of gear shall drive him forth and hunger arm
his hand,
To win his food from the desert rude, his pittance from
the sand.
His neighbours' smoke shall vex his eyes, their voices
break his rest.
He shall go forth till south is north sullen and dis-
possessed.
He shall desire loneliness and his desire shall bring,
Hard on his heels, a thousand wheels, a People and a
King.
He shall come back on his own track, and by his scarce-
cooled camp
There shall he meet the roaring street, the derrick and
the stamp:
There shall he blaze a nation's ways with hatchet and
with brand,
Till on his last-won wilderness an Empire's outposts
stand.

A SCHOOL SONG

'LET us now praise famous men'—
    Men of little showing—
For their work continueth,
And their work continueth,
Broad and deep continueth,
    Greater than their knowing!

Western wind and open surge
    Took us from our mothers,
Flung us on a naked shore
(Twelve bleak houses by the shore!
Seven summers by the shore!)
    'Mid two hundred brothers.

There we met with famous men
    Set in office o'er us;
And they beat on us with rods—
Faithfully with many rods—
Daily beat us on with rods,
    For the love they bore us!

Out of Egypt unto Troy—
    Over Himalaya—
Far and sure our bands have gone—
Hy-Brasil or Babylon,
Islands of the Southern Run,
    And Cities of Cathaia!

114

A SCHOOL SONG

And we all praise famous men—
  Ancients of the College;
For they taught us common sense—
Tried to teach us common sense—
Truth and God's Own Common Sense,
  Which is more than knowledge!

Each degree of Latitude
  Strung about Creation
Seeth one or more of us
(Of one muster each of us),
Diligent in that he does,
  Keen in his vocation.

This we learned from famous men,
  Knowing not its uses,
When they showed, in daily work,
Man must finish off his work—
Right or wrong, his daily work—
  And without excuses.

Servants of the Staff and chain,
  Mine and fuse and grapnel—
Some before the face of Kings,
Stand before the face of Kings;
Bearing gifts to divers Kings—
  Gifts of case and shrapnel.

This we learned from famous men
  Teaching in our borders,
Who declared it was best,
Safest, easiest, and best—
Expeditious, wise, and best—
  To obey your orders.

Some beneath the farther stars
   Bear the greater burden:
Set to serve the lands they rule,
(Save he serve no man may rule),
Serve and love the lands they rule;
   Seeking praise nor guerdon.

This we learned from famous men,
   Knowing not we learned it.
Only, as the years went by—
Lonely, as the years went by—
Far from help as years went by,
   Plainer we discerned it.

Wherefore praise we famous men
   From whose bays we borrow—
They that put aside To-day—
All the joys of their To-day—
And with toil of their To-day
   Bought for us To-morrow!

Bless and praise we famous men—
   Men of little showing—
For their work continueth,
And their work continueth,
Broad and deep continueth,
   Great beyond their knowing!

THE LAW OF THE JUNGLE

NOW this is the Law of the Jungle—as old and as
true as the sky;
And the Wolf that shall keep it may prosper, but
the Wolf that shall break it must die.

As the creeper that girdles the tree-trunk the Law run-
neth forward and back—
For the strength of the Pack is the Wolf, and the strength
of the Wolf is the Pack.

Wash daily from nose-tip to tail-tip; drink deeply, but
never too deep;
And remember the night is for hunting, and forget not
the day is for sleep.

The Jackal may follow the Tiger, but, Cub, when thy
whiskers are grown,
Remember the Wolf is a hunter—go forth and get food
of thine own.

Keep peace with the Lords of the Jungle—the Tiger, the
Panther, the Bear;
And trouble not Hathi the Silent, and mock not the
Boar in his lair.

117

When Pack meets with Pack in the Jungle, and neither
    will go from the trail,
Lie down till the leaders have spoken—it may be fair
    words shall prevail.

When ye fight with a Wolf of the Pack, ye must fight him
    alone and afar,
Lest others take part in the quarrel, and the Pack be
    diminished by war.

The Lair of the Wolf is his refuge, and where he has
    made him his home,
Not even the Head Wolf may enter, not even the Coun-
    cil may come.

The Lair of the Wolf is his refuge, but where he has
    digged it too plain,
The Council shall send him a message, and so he shall
    change it again.

If ye kill before midnight, be silent, and wake not the
    woods with your bay,
Lest ye frighten the deer from the crops, and the brothers
    go empty away.

Ye may kill for yourselves, and your mates, and your
    cubs as they need, and ye can;
But kill not for pleasure of killing, and seven times
    never kill Man!

If ye plunder his Kill from a weaker, devour not all in
    thy pride;
Pack-Right is the right of the meanest; so leave him the
    head and the hide.

THE LAW OF THE JUNGLE

The Kill of the Pack is the meat of the Pack.   Ye must
    eat where it lies;
And no one may carry away of that meat to his lair, or
    he dies.

The Kill of the Wolf is the meat of the Wolf.   He may
    do what he will,
But, till he has given permission, the Pack may not eat
    of that Kill.

Cub-Right is the right of the Yearling.   From all of his
    Pack he may claim
Full-gorge when the killer has eaten; and none may refuse
    him the same.

Lair-Right is the right of the Mother.   From all of her
    year she may claim
One haunch of each kill for her litter; and none may deny
    her the same.

Cave-Right is the right of the Father—to hunt by him-
    self for his own:
He is freed of all calls to the Pack; he is judged by the
    Council alone.

Because of his age and his cunning, because of his gripe
    and his paw,
In all that the Law leaveth open, the word of the Head
    Wolf is Law.

Now these are the Laws of the Jungle, and many and
    mighty are they;
But the head and the hoof of the Law and the haunch
    and the hump is—Obey!

'A SERVANT WHEN HE REIGNETH'

(For three things the earth is disquieted, and for four which it cannot bear. For a servant when he reigneth, and a fool when he is filled with meat; for an odious woman when she is married, and an handmaid that is heir to her mistress.—Prov. xxx. 21–23.)

THREE things make earth unquiet,
 And four she cannot brook;
 The godly Agur counted them
 And put them in a book—
Those Four Tremendous Curses
 With which mankind is cursed:
But a Servant when he Reigneth
 Old Agur counted first.

An Handmaid that is Mistress
 We need not call upon,
A Fool when he is full of Meat
 Will fall asleep anon.
An Odious Woman Married
 May bear a babe and mend,
But a Servant when He Reigneth
 Is Confusion to the end.

His feet are swift to tumult,
 His hands are slow to toil,
His ears are deaf to reason,
 His lips are loud in broil.

'A SERVANT WHEN HE REIGNETH'

He knows no use for power
    Except to show his might,
He gives no heed to judgment
    Unless it prove him right.

Because he served a master
    Before his Kingship came,
And hid in all disaster
    Behind his master's name.
So, when his Folly opens
    The unnecessary hells,
A Servant when He Reigneth
    Throws the blame on some one else.

His vows are lightly spoken,
    His faith is hard to bind,
His trust is easy broken,
    He fears his fellow-kind.
The nearest mob will move him
    To break the pledge he gave—
Oh a Servant when He Reigneth
    Is more than ever slave!

The...
Or...

MY FATHER'S CHAIR

THERE are four good legs to my Father's Chair—
 Priest and People and Lords and Crown.
 I sit on all of 'em fair and square,
  And that is the reason it don't break down.

I won't trust one leg, nor two, nor three,
 To carry my weight when I sit me down,
I want all four of 'em under me—
 Priest and People and Lords and Crown.

I sit on all four and I favour none—
 Priest, nor People, nor Lords, nor Crown—
And I never tilt in my chair, my son,
  And that is the reason it don't break down!

When your time comes to sit in my Chair,
 Remember your Father's habits and rules,
Sit on all four legs, fair and square,
  And never be tempted by one-legged stools!

Excellent

Down

'OUR FATHERS OF OLD'

EXCELLENT herbs had our fathers of old—
    Excellent herbs to ease their pain—
    Alexanders and Marigold,
        Eyebright, Orris, and Elecampane.
Basil, Rocket, Valerian, Rue
    (Almost singing themselves they run),
Vervain, Dittany, Call-me-to-you—
    Cowslip, Melilot, Rose of the Sun.
        Anything green that grew out of the mould
        Was an excellent herb to our fathers of old.

Wonderful tales had our fathers of old—
    Wonderful tales of the herbs and the stars—
The Sun was Lord of the Marigold,
    Basil and Rocket belonged to Mars.
Pat as a sum in division it goes—
    (Every plant had a star bespoke)—
Who but Venus should govern the Rose?
    Who but Jupiter own the Oak?
        Simply and gravely the facts are told
        In the wonderful books of our fathers of old.

Wonderful little, when all is said,
    Wonderful little our fathers knew.
Half their remedies cured you dead—
    Most of their teaching was quite untrue—

'Look at the stars when a patient is ill
　(Dirt has nothing to do with disease),
Bleed and blister as much as you will,
　Blister and bleed him as oft as you please.'
　　Whence enormous and manifold
　　Errors were made by our fathers of old.

Yet when the sickness was sore in the land,
　And neither planets nor herbs assuaged,
They took their lives in their lancet-hand
　And, oh, what a wonderful war they waged!
Yes, when the crosses were chalked on the door—
　(Yes, when the terrible dead-cart rolled),
Excellent courage our fathers bore—
　Excellent heart had our fathers of old.
　　None too learned, but nobly bold
　　Into the fight went our fathers of old.

If it be certain, as Galen says,
　And sage Hippocrates holds as much—
'That those afflicted by doubts and dismays
　Are mightily helped by a dead man's touch,'
Then, be good to us, stars above!
　Then, be good to us, herbs below!
We are afflicted by what we can prove,
　We are distracted by what we know.
　　So—ah, so!
　　Down from your heaven or up from your mould,
　Send us the hearts of our fathers of old!

BEFORE EDGEHILL

October, 1642

Naked and gray the Cotswolds stand
    Beneath the autumn sun,
  And the stubble fields on either hand
    Where Stour and Avon run,
There is no change in the patient land
  That has bred us every one.

She should have passed in cloud and fire
    And saved us from this sin
Of war—red war—'twixt child and sire,
    Household and kith and kin,
In the heart of a sleepy Midland shire,
    With the harvest scarcely in.

But there is no change as we meet at last
    On the brow-head or the plain,
And the raw astonished ranks stand fast
    To slay or to be slain
By the men they knew in the kindly past
    That shall never come again—

By the men they met at dance or chase,
    In the tavern or the hall,
At the justice-bench and the market-place,

At the cudgel-play or brawl,
Of their own blood and speech and race,
Comrades or neighbours all!

More bitter than death this day must prove
Whichever way it go,
For the brothers of the maids we love
Make ready to lay low
Their sisters' sweethearts, as we move
Against our dearest foe.

Thank Heaven! At last the trumpets peal
Before our strength gives way.
For King or for the Commonweal
No matter which they say,
The first dry rattle of new-drawn steel
Changes the world to-day!

SONGS FROM BOOKS

THE HERITAGE

OUR Fathers in a wondrous age,
    Ere yet the Earth was small,
    Ensured to us an heritage,
    And doubted not at all
That we, the children of their heart,
    Which then did beat so high,
In later time should play like part
    For our posterity.

A thousand years they steadfast built,
    To 'vantage us and ours,
The Walls that were a world's despair,
    The sea-constraining Towers:
Yet in their midmost pride they knew,
    And unto Kings made known,
Not all from these their strength they drew,
    Their faith from brass or stone.

Youth's passion, manhood's fierce intent,
    With age's judgment wise,
They spent, and counted not they spent,
    At daily sacrifice.
Not lambs alone nor purchased doves
    Or tithe of trader's gold—
Their lives most dear, their dearer loves,
    They offered up of old.

Refraining e'en from lawful things,
  They bowed the neck to bear
The unadorned yoke that brings
  Stark toil and sternest care.
Wherefore through them is Freedom sure;
  Wherefore through them we stand
From all but sloth and pride secure,
  In a delightsome land.

Then, fretful, murmur not they gave
  So great a charge to keep,
Nor dream that awestruck Time shall save
  Their labour while we sleep.
Dear-bought and clear, a thousand year,
  Our fathers' title runs.
Make we likewise their sacrifice,
  Defrauding not our sons.

THE RIVER'S TALE

TWENTY bridges from Tower to Kew
Wanted to know what the River knew,
For they were young and the Thames was old,
And this is the tale that the River told:—

'I walk my beat before London Town,
Five hours up and seven down.
Up I go and I end my run
At Tide-end-town, which is Teddington.
Down I come with the mud in my hands
And plaster it over the Maplin Sands.
But I'd have you know that these waters of mine
Were once a branch of the River Rhine,
When hundreds of miles to the East I went
And England was joined to the Continent.

'I remember the bat-winged lizard-birds,
The Age of Ice and the mammoth herds,
And the giant tigers that stalked them down
Through Regent's Park into Camden Town.
And I remember like yesterday
The earliest Cockney who came my way,
When he pushed through the forest that lined the Strand,
With paint on his face and a club in his hand.
He was death to feather and fin and fur,
He trapped my beavers at Westminster,

He netted my salmon, he hunted my deer,
He killed my herons off Lambeth Pier;
He fought his neighbour with axes and swords,
Flint or bronze, at my upper fords,
While down at Greenwich for slaves and tin
The tall Phœnician ships stole in,
And North Sea war-boats, painted and gay,
Flashed like dragon-flies Erith way;
And Norseman and Negro and Gaul and Greek
Drank with the Britons in Barking Creek,
And life was gay, and the world was new,
And I was a mile across at Kew!
But the Roman came with a heavy hand,
And bridged and roaded and ruled the land,
And the Roman left and the Danes blew in—
And that's where your history books begin!'

SONG OF THE FIFTH RIVER

WHEN first by Eden Tree,
The Four Great Rivers ran,
To each was appointed a Man
Her Prince and Ruler to be.

But after this was ordained
(The ancient legends tell),
There came dark Israel,
For whom no River remained.

Then He Whom the Rivers obey
Said to him: 'Fling on the ground
A handful of yellow clay,
And a Fifth Great River shall run,
Mightier than these Four,
In secret the Earth around;
And Her secret evermore,
Shall be shown to thee and thy Race.'

So it was said and done.
And, deep in the veins of Earth,
And, fed by a thousand springs
That comfort the market-place,

131

Or sap the power of Kings,
The Fifth Great River had birth,
Even as it was foretold—
The Secret River of Gold!

And Israel laid down
His sceptre and his crown,
To brood on that River bank,
Where the waters flashed and sank,
And burrowed in earth and fell,
And bided a season below,
For reason that none might know,
Save only Israel.

He is Lord of the Last—
The Fifth, most wonderful, Flood.
He hears Her thunder past
And Her Song is in his blood.
He can foresay: 'She will fall,'
For he knows which fountain dries
Behind which desert-belt
A thousand leagues to the South.

He can foresay: 'She will rise.'
He knows what far snows melt
Along what mountain-wall
A thousand leagues to the North.
He snuffs the coming drouth
As he snuffs the coming rain,
He knows what each will bring forth,
And turns it to his gain.

SONG OF THE FIFTH RIVER

A Ruler without a Throne,
A Prince without a Sword,
Israel follows his quest.
In every land a guest,
Of many lands a lord,
In no land King is he.
But the Fifth Great River keeps
The secret of Her deeps
For Israel alone,
As it was ordered to be.

THE CHILDREN'S SONG

LAND of our Birth, we pledge to thee
    Our love and toil in the years to be;
    When we are grown and take our place,
As men and women with our race.

Father in Heaven who lovest all,
Oh help Thy children when they call;
That they may build from age to age,
An undefiled heritage.

Teach us to bear the yoke in youth,
With steadfastness and careful truth;
That, in our time, Thy Grace may give
The Truth whereby the Nations live.

Teach us to rule ourselves alway,
Controlled and cleanly night and day;
That we may bring, if need arise,
No maimed or worthless sacrifice.

Teach us to look in all our ends,
On Thee for judge, and not our friends;
That we, with Thee, may walk uncowed
By fear or favour of the crowd.

THE CHILDREN'S SONG

Teach us the Strength that cannot seek,
By deed or thought, to hurt the weak;
That, under Thee, we may possess
Man's strength to comfort man's distress.

Teach us Delight in simple things,
And Mirth that has no bitter springs;
Forgiveness free of evil done,
And Love to all men 'neath the sun!

Land of our Birth, our faith, our pride,
For whose dear sake our fathers died;
O Motherland, we pledge to thee,
Head, heart, and hand through the years to be!

PARADE–SONG OF THE CAMP–ANIMALS

Elephants of the Gun–Teams

WE lent to Alexander the strength of Hercules,
The wisdom of our foreheads, the cunning of
our knees.
We bowed our necks to service; they ne'er were loosed
again,—
Make way there, way for the ten-foot teams
Of the Forty-Pounder train!

Gun–Bullocks

Those heroes in their harnesses avoid a cannon-ball,
And what they know of powder upsets them one and
all;
Then we come into action and tug the guns again,—
Make way there, way for the twenty yoke
Of the Forty-Pounder train!

Cavalry Horses

By the brand on my withers, the finest of tunes
Is played by the Lancers, Hussars, and Dragoons,
And it's sweeter than 'Stables' or 'Water' to me,
The Cavalry Canter of 'Bonnie Dundee'!

PARADE–SONG OF THE CAMP–ANIMALS

Then feed us and break us and handle and groom,
And give us good riders and plenty of room,
And launch us in column of squadron and see
The Way of the War-horse to 'Bonnie Dundee'!

Screw–Gun Mules

As me and my companions were scrambling up a hill,
The path was lost in rolling stones, but we went forward
    still;
For we can wriggle and climb, my lads, and turn up
    everywhere,
And it's our delight on a mountain height, with a leg or
    two to spare!

Good luck to every sergeant, then, that lets us pick our
    road!
Bad luck to all the driver-men that cannot pack a load!
For we can wriggle and climb, my lads, and turn up
    everywhere,
And it's our delight on a mountain height, with a leg or
    two to spare!

Commissariat Camels

We haven't a camelty tune of our own
    To help us trollop along,
But every neck is a hair-trombone
    (Rtt-ta-ta-ta! is a hair-trombone!)
And this is our marching-song:
    Can't! Don't! Shan't! Won't!
Pass it along the line!

137

Somebody's pack has slid from his back,
'Wish it were only mine!
Somebody's load has tipped off in the road—
Cheer for a halt and a row!
Urrr! Yarrh! Grr! Arrh!
Somebody's catching it now!

All the Beasts Together

Children of the Camp are we,
Serving each in his degree;
Children of the yoke and goad,
Pack and harness, pad and load.
See our line across the plain,
Like a heel-rope bent again,
Reaching, writhing, rolling far,
Sweeping all away to war!
While the men that walk beside,
Dusty, silent, heavy-eyed,
Cannot tell why we or they
March and suffer day by day.
　　Children of the Camp are we,
　　Serving each in his degree;
　　Children of the yoke and goad,
　　Pack and harness, pad and load.

CHAPTER HEADINGS

Beast and Man in India

THEY killed a child to please the Gods
    In earth's young penitence,
And I have bled in that Babe's stead
    Because of innocence.

I bear the sins of sinful men
    That have no sin of my own;
They drive me forth to Heaven's wrath
    Unpastured and alone.

I am the meat of sacrifice,
    The ransom of man's guilt,
For they give my life to the altar knife
    Wherever shrine is built.

                    'The Goat.'

Between the waving tufts of jungle-grass,
Up from the river as the twilight falls,
Across the dust-beclouded plain they pass
    On to the village walls.

Great is the sword and mighty is the pen,
But greater far the labouring ploughman's blade,
For on its oxen and its husbandmen
    An Empire's strength is laid.

                    'The Oxen.'

The torn boughs trailing o'er the tusks aslant,
  The saplings reeling in the path he trod,
Declare his might—our lord the Elephant,
  Chief of the ways of God.

The black bulk heaving where the oxen pant,
  The bowed head toiling where the guns careen,
Declare our might—our slave the Elephant,
  And servant of the Queen.

'The Elephant.'

Dark children of the mere and marsh,
  Wallow and waste and lea;
Outcaste they wait at the village gate
  With folk of low degree.

Their pasture is in no man's land,
  Their food the cattle's scorn;
Their rest is mire and their desire
  The thicket and the thorn.

But woe to those who break their sleep,
  And woe to those who dare
To rouse the herd-bull from his keep,
  The wild boar from his lair!

'Pigs and Buffaloes.'

The beasts are very wise,
Their mouths are clean of lies;
They talk one to the other,
Bullock to bullock's brother
Resting after their labours,
Each in stall with his neighbours.
But man with goad and whip,
Breaks up their fellowship,

Shouts in their silky ears
Filling their souls with fears,
When he has ploughed the land,
He says:—'They understand.'
But the beasts in stall together,
Freed from the yoke and tether,
Say as the torn flanks smoke—
'Nay, 'twas the whip that spoke.'

Life's Handicap

There's a convict more in the Central Jail
    Behind the old mud wall;
There's a lifter less on the Border trail,
    And the Queen's peace over all,
                Dear boys,
    The Queen's peace over all!

For we must bear our leader's blame,
    On us the shame will fall,
If we lift our hand from a fettered land
    And the Queen's peace over all,
                Dear boys,
    The Queen's peace over all!
                'The Head of the District.'

The doors were wide, the story saith,
Out of the night came the patient wraith,
He might not speak and he could not stir
A hair of the Baron's minniver.
Speechless and strengthless a shadow thin,
He roved the castle to find his kin.

And oh! 'twas a piteous sight to see
The dumb ghost follow his enemy!
                                    'The Return of Imray.'

Before my Spring I garnered Autumn's gain,
Out of her time my field was white with grain,
    The year gave up her secrets, to my woe.
Forced and deflowered each sick season lay,
In mystery of increase and decay.
I saw the sunset ere men see the day,
    Who am too wise in all I should not know.
                                    'Without Benefit of Clergy.'

Many Inventions

And if ye doubt the tale I tell,
Steer through the South Pacific swell;
Go where the branching coral hives
Unending strife of endless lives,
Where, leagued about the 'wildered boat,
The rainbow jellies fill and float;
And, lilting where the laver lingers,
The starfish trips on all her fingers;
Where, 'neath his myriad spines ashock,
The sea-egg ripples down the rock,
An orange wonder dimly guessed,
From darkness where the cuttles rest,
Moored o'er the darker deeps that hide
The blind white Sea-snake and his bride
Who, drowsing, nose the long-lost ships
Let down through darkness to their lips.
                                    'A Matter of Fact.'

CHAPTER HEADINGS

'Less you want your toes trod off you'd better get back
    at once,
    For the bullocks are walkin' two by two,
    The byles are walkin' two by two,
    The bullocks are walkin' two by two,
And the elephants bring the guns.
      Ho! Yuss!

Great—big—long—black—forty-pounder guns:
    Jiggery-jolty to and fro,
    Each as big as a launch in tow—
Blind—dumb—broad-breeched—beggars o' battering-
    guns.
                  'My Lord the Elephant.'

All the world over, nursing their scars,
Sit the old fighting-men broke in the wars—
Sit the old fighting-men, surly and grim,
Mocking the lilt of the conquerors' hymn.

Dust of the battle o'erwhelmed them and hid.
Fame never found them for aught that they did.
Wounded and spent to the lazar they drew,
Lining the road where the Legions roll through.

Sons of the Laurel who press to your meed,
(Worthy God's pity most—ye who succeed!)
Ere you go triumphing, crowned, to the stars,
Pity poor fighting men, broke in the wars!
                    'Collected.'

Kim

Unto whose use the pregnant suns are poised
　With idiot moons and stars retracting stars?
Creep thou between—thy coming's all unnoised.
　Heaven hath her high, as Earth her baser, wars.
Heir to these tumults, this affright, that fray
(By Adam's, father's, own, sin bound alway);
Peer up, draw out thy horoscope and say
　Which planet mends thy threadbare fate, or mar

OUTSONG IN THE JUNGLE

Baloo

FOR the sake of him who showed
One wise Frog the Jungle-Road,
Keep the Law the Man-Pack make—
For thy blind old Baloo's sake!
Clean or tainted, hot or stale,
Hold it as it were the Trail,
Through the day and through the night,
Questing neither left nor right.
For the sake of him who loves
Thee beyond all else that moves,
When thy Pack would make thee pain,
Say: 'Tabaqui sings again.'
When thy Pack would work thee ill,
Say: 'Shere Khan is yet to kill.'
When the knife is drawn to slay,
Keep the Law and go thy way.
(Root and honey, palm and spathe,
Guard a cub from harm and scathe!)
Wood and Water, Wind and Tree,
Jungle-Favour go with thee!

Kaa

Anger is the egg of Fear—
Only lidless eyes are clear.

147

Cobra-poison none may leech.
Even so with Cobra-speech.
Open talk shall call to thee
Strength, whose mate is Courtesy.
Send no lunge beyond thy length;
Lend no rotten bough thy strength.
Gauge thy gape with buck or goat,
Lest thine eye should choke thy throat.
After gorging, wouldst thou sleep?
Look thy den be hid and deep,
Lest a wrong, by thee forgot,
Draw thy killer to the spot.
East and West and North and South,
Wash thy hide and close thy mouth.
(Pit and rift and blue pool-brim,
Middle-Jungle follow him!)
Wood and Water, Wind and Tree,
Jungle-Favour go with thee!

Bagheera

In the cage my life began;
Well I know the worth of Man.
By the Broken Lock that freed—
Man-cub, 'ware the Man-cub's breed!
Scenting-dew or starlight pale,
Choose no tangled tree-cat trail.
Pack or council, hunt or den,
Cry no truce with Jackal-Men.
Feed them silence when they say:
'Come with us an easy way.'
Feed them silence when they seek
Help of thine to hurt the weak.

OUTSONG IN THE JUNGLE

Make no bandar's boast of skill;
Hold thy peace above the kill.
Let nor call nor song nor sign
Turn thee from thy hunting-line.
(Morning mist or twilight clear,
Serve him, Wardens of the Deer!)
Wood and Water, Wind and Tree,
Jungle-Favour go with thee!

The Three

On the trail that thou must tread
To the thresholds of our dread,
Where the Flower blossoms red;
Through the nights when thou shalt lie
Prisoned from our Mother-sky,
Hearing us, thy loves, go by;
In the dawns when thou shalt wake
To the toil thou canst not break,
Heartsick for the Jungle's sake:
Wood and Water, Wind and Tree,
Wisdom, Strength, and Courtesy,
Jungle-Favour go with thee!

149

THE PRODIGAL SON

(Western Version)

HERE come I to my own again,
    Fed, forgiven and known again,
    Claimed by bone of my bone again,
And cheered by flesh of my flesh.
The fatted calf is dressed for me,
But the husks have greater zest for me,
I think my pigs will be best for me,
    So I'm off to the Yards afresh.

I never was very refined, you see
(And it weighs on my brother's mind, you see),
But there's no reproach among swine, d'you see,
    For being a bit of a swine.
So I'm off with wallet and staff to eat
The bread that is three parts chaff to wheat,
But glory be!—there's a laugh to it,
    Which isn't the case when we dine.

My father glooms and advises me,
My brother sulks and despises me,
And Mother catechises me
    Till I want to go out and swear.

THE PRODIGAL SON

And, in spite of the butler's gravity,
I know that the servants have it I
Am a monster of moral depravity,
    And I'm damned if I think it's fair!

I wasted my substance, I know I did,
On riotous living, so I did,
But there's nothing on record to show I did
    Worse than my betters have done.
They talk of the money I spent out there—
They hint at the pace that I went out there—
But they all forget I was sent out there
    Alone as a rich man's son.

So I was a mark for plunder at once,
And lost my cash (can you wonder?) at once,
But I didn't give up and knock under at once,
    I worked in the Yards, for a spell,
Where I spent my nights and my days with hogs,
And shared their milk and maize with hogs,
Till, I guess, I have learned what pays with hogs
    And—I have that knowledge to sell!

So back I go to my job again,
Not so easy to rob again,
Or quite so ready to sob again
    On any neck that's around.
I'm leaving, Pater. Good-bye to you!
God bless you, Mater! I'll write to you. . . .
I wouldn't be impolite to you,
    But, Brother, you are a hound!

A SONG OF KABIR

OH, light was the world that he weighed in his hands!
    Oh, heavy the tale of his fiefs and his lands!
He has gone from the guddee and put on the shroud,
And departed in guise of bairagi avowed!

Now the white road to Delhi is mat for his feet.
The sal and the kikar must guard him from heat.
His home is the camp, and the waste, and the crowd—
He is seeking the Way as bairagi avowed!

He has looked upon Man, and his eyeballs are clear—
(There was One; there is One, and but One, saith Kabir);
The Red Mist of Doing has thinned to a cloud—
He has taken the Path for bairagi avowed!

To learn and discern of his brother the clod,
Of his brother the brute, and his brother the God,
He has gone from the council and put on the shroud
('Can ye hear?' saith Kabir), a bairagi avowed!

THE NECESSITARIAN

I KNOW not in Whose hands are laid
   To empty upon earth
From unsuspected ambuscade
   The very Urns of Mirth;

Who bids the Heavenly Lark arise
   And cheer our solemn round—
The Jest beheld with streaming eyes
   And grovellings on the ground;

Who joins the flats of Time and Chance
   Behind the prey preferred,
And thrones on Shrieking Circumstance
   The Sacredly Absurd,

Till Laughter, voiceless through excess,
   Waves mute appeal and sore,
Above the midriff's deep distress,
   For breath to laugh once more.

No creed hath dared to hail Him Lord,
   No raptured choirs proclaim,
And Nature's strenuous Overword
   Hath nowhere breathed His Name.

Yet, it must be, on wayside jape
    The selfsame Power bestows
The selfsame power as went to shape
    His Planet or His Rose.

THE JESTER

THERE are three degrees of bliss
    At the foot of Allah's Throne,
    And the highest place is his
Who saves a brother's soul
At peril of his own;
There is the Power made known!

There are three degrees of bliss
In the Gardens of Paradise,
And the second place is his
Who saves his brother's soul
By excellent advice.
For there the Glory lies!

There are three degrees of bliss
And three abodes of the Blest,
And the lowest place is his
Who has saved a soul by a jest
And a brother's soul in sport . . .
But there do the Angels resort!

A SONG OF TRAVEL

WHERE'S the lamp that Hero lit
    Once to call Leander home?
    Equal Time hath shovelled it
'Neath the wrack of Greece and Rome.
Neither wait we any more
That worn sail which Argo bore.

Dust and dust of ashes close
    All the Vestal Virgins' care;
And the oldest altar shows
    But an older darkness there.
Age-encamped Oblivion
Tenteth every light that shone!

Yet shall we, for Suns that die,
    Wall our wanderings from desire?
Or, because the Moon is high,
    Scorn to use a nearer fire?
Lest some envious Pharaoh stir,
Make our lives our sepulchre?

Nay! Though Time with petty Fate
    Prison us and Emperors,
By our Arts do we create
    That which Time himself devours—
Such machines as well may run
'Gainst the horses of the Sun.

A SONG OF TRAVEL

When we would a new abode,
   Space, our tyrant King no more,
Lays the long lance of the road
   At our feet and flees before,
Breathless, ere we overwhelm,
To submit a further realm!

A SONG OF TRAVEL

When we *would* seek a new abode,
Space out before Kong-hó more
Bars the bleak limbs of the road,
About feed and thus before,
Deathless, *we* we even being,
To satis...

THE TWO–SIDED MAN

MUCH I owe to the Land that grew—
　　More to the Life that fed—
　　But most to Allah Who gave me two
　　Separate sides to my head.

Much I reflect on the Good and the True
　　In the Faiths beneath the sun,
But most upon Allah Who gave me two
　　Sides to my head, not one.

Wesley's following, Calvin's flock,
　　White or yellow or bronze,
Shaman, Ju-ju or Angekok,
　　Minister, Mukamuk, Bonze—

Here is a health, my brothers, to you,
　　However your prayers are said,
And praised be Allah Who gave me two
　　Separate sides to my head!

I would go without shirt or shoe,
　　Friend, tobacco or bread,
Sooner than lose for a minute the two
　　Separate sides of my head!

'LUKANNON'

(Song of the breeding Seal.   Aleutian Islands)

MET my mates in the morning (and oh, but I am
  old!)
Where roaring on the ledges the summer ground-
  swell rolled.
heard them lift the chorus that drowned the breakers'
  song—
he Beaches of Lukannon—two million voices strong!

he song of pleasant stations beside the salt lagoons,
he song of blowing squadrons that shuffled down the
  dunes,
he song of midnight dances that churned the sea to
  flame—
he Beaches of Lukannon—before the sealers came!

met my mates in the morning (I'll never meet them
  more!);
hey came and went in legions that darkened all the
  shore.
nd through the foam-flecked offing as far as voice
  could reach
/e hailed the landing-parties and we sang them up the
  beach.

The Beaches of Lukannon—the winter-wheat so tall—
The dripping, crinkled lichens, and the sea-fog drench
  ing all!
The platforms of our playground, all shining smooth an
  worn!
The Beaches of Lukannon—the home where we wer
  born!

I meet my mates in the morning, a broken, scattere
  band.
Men shoot us in the water and club us on the land;
Men drive us to the Salt House like silly sheep and tame
And still we sing Lukannon—before the sealers came.

Wheel down, wheel down to southward! Oh, Goover
  ooska go!
And tell the Deep-Sea Viceroys the story of our woe;
Ere, empty as the shark's egg the tempest flings ashor
The Beaches of Lukannon shall know their sons no more

AN ASTROLOGER'S SONG

TO the Heavens above us
    O look and behold
    The Planets that love us
    All harnessed in gold!
What chariots, what horses
    Against us shall bide
While the Stars in their courses
    Do fight on our side?

All thought, all desires,
    That are under the sun,
Are one with their fires,
    As we also are one.
All matter, all spirit,
    All fashion, all frame,
Receive and inherit
    Their strength from the same.

Oh, man that deniest
    All power save thine own,
Their power in the highest
    Is mightily shown.
Not less in the lowest
    That power is made clear.
(Oh, man, if thou knowest,
    What treasure is here!)

Earth quakes in her throes,
  And we wonder for why.
But the blind planet knows
  When her ruler is nigh;
And, attuned since Creation
  To perfect accord,
She thrills in her station
  And yearns to her Lord.

The waters have risen,
  The springs are unbound—
The floods break their prison,
  And ravin around.
No rampart withstands 'em,
  Their fury will last,
Till the Sign that commands 'em
  Sinks low or swings past.

Through abysses unproven,
  O'er gulfs beyond thought,
Our portion is woven,
  Our burden is brought.
Yet They that prepare it,
  Whose Nature we share,
Make us who must bear it
  Well able to bear.

Though terrors o'ertake us
  We'll not be afraid.
No Power can unmake us
  Save that which has made.

AN ASTROLOGER'S SONG

Nor yet beyond reason
  Or hope shall we fall—
All things have their season,
  And Mercy crowns all!

Then, doubt not, ye fearful—
  The Eternal is King—
Up, heart, and be cheerful,
  And lustily sing:—
What chariots, what horses,
  Against us shall bide
While the Stars in their courses
  Do fight on our side?

'THE POWER OF THE DOG'

THERE is sorrow enough in the natural way
From men and women to fill our day;
But when we are certain of sorrow in store,
Why do we always arrange for more?
Brothers and Sisters, I bid you beware
Of giving your heart to a dog to tear.

Buy a pup and your money will buy
Love unflinching that cannot lie—
Perfect passion and worship fed
By a kick in the ribs or a pat on the head.
Nevertheless, it is hardly fair
To risk your heart for a dog to tear.

When the fourteen years which Nature permits
Are closing in asthma, or tumour, or fits,
And the vet's unspoken prescription runs
To lethal chambers or loaded guns,
Then you will find—it's your own affair,
But . . . you've given your heart to a dog to tear.

When the body that lived at your single will,
When the whimper of welcome, is stilled (how still!),
When the spirit that answered your every mood
Is gone—wherever it goes—for good,
You will discover how much you care,
And will give your heart to a dog to tear.

'THE POWER OF THE DOG'

We've sorrow enough in the natural way,
When it comes to burying Christian clay.
Our loves are not given, but only lent,
At compound interest of cent per cent.
Though it is not always the case, I believe,
That the longer we've kept 'em, the more do we grieve:
For, when debts are payable, right or wrong,
A short-time loan is as bad as a long—
So why in—Heaven (before we are there)
Should we give our hearts to a dog to tear?

THE RABBI'S SONG

IF Thought can reach to Heaven,
    On Heaven let it dwell,
  For fear thy Thought be given
    Like power to reach to Hell.
For fear the desolation
  And darkness of thy mind
Perplex an habitation
  Which thou hast left behind.

Let nothing linger after—
  No whimpering ghost remain,
In wall, or beam, or rafter,
  Of any hate or pain.
Cleanse and call home thy spirit,
  Deny her leave to cast,
On aught thy heirs inherit,
  The shadow of her past.

For think, in all thy sadness,
  What road our griefs may take;
Whose brain reflect our madness,
  Or whom our terrors shake.
For think, lest any languish
  By cause of thy distress—
The arrows of our anguish
  Fly farther than we guess.

THE RABBI'S SONG

Our lives, our tears, as water,
   Are spilled upon the ground;
God giveth no man quarter,
   Yet God a means hath found,
Though faith and hope have vanished,
   And even love grows dim—
A means whereby His banished
   Be not expelled from Him.

THE BEE BOY'S SONG

BEES! Bees! Hark to your bees!
'Hide from your neighbours as much as you please,
But all that has happened, to us you must tell,
Or else we will give you no honey to sell!'

A maiden in her glory,
   Upon her wedding-day,
Must tell her Bees the story,
   Or else they'll fly away.
         Fly away—die away—
            Dwindle down and leave you!
         But if you don't deceive your Bees,
            Your Bees will not deceive you.

Marriage, birth or buryin',
   News across the seas,
All you're sad or merry in,
   You must tell the Bees,
         Tell 'em coming in an' out,
            Where the Fanners fan,
         'Cause the Bees are just about
            As curious as a man!

Don't you wait where trees are,
   When the lightnings play,
Nor don't you hate where Bees are,
   Or else they'll pine away.

THE BEE BOY'S SONG

Pine away—dwine away—
Anything to leave you!
But if you never grieve your Bees,
Your Bees 'll never grieve you.

THE RETURN OF THE CHILDREN

NEITHER the harps nor the crowns amused, nor
the cherubs' dove-winged races—
  Holding hands forlornly the Children wandered
  beneath the Dome,
Plucking the radiant robes of the passers-by, and with
pitiful faces
Begging what Princes and Powers refused:—'Ah, please
will you let us go home?'

Over the jewelled floor, nigh weeping, ran to them Mary
the Mother,
Kneeled and caressed and made promise with kisses, and
drew them along to the gateway—
Yea, the all-iron unbribeable Door which Peter must
guard and none other.
Straightway She took the Keys from his keeping, and
opened and freed them straightway.

Then, to Her Son, Who had seen and smiled, She said:
'On the night that I bore Thee,
What didst Thou care for a love beyond mine or a
heaven that was not my arm?
Didst Thou push from the nipple, O Child, to hear the
angels adore Thee?
When we two lay in the breath of the kine?'   And He
said:—'Thou hast done no harm.'

through the Void the Children ran homeward merrily
hand in hand,

ooking neither to left nor right where the breathless
Heavens stood still;

nd the Guards of the Void resheathed their swords, for
they heard the Command:

hall I that have suffered the children to come to Me
hold them against their will?'

MERROW DOWN

I

THERE runs a road by Merrow Down—
 A grassy track to-day it is—
An hour out of Guildford town,
 Above the river Wey it is.

Here, when they heard the horse-bells ring,
 The ancient Britons dressed and rode
To watch the dark Phœnicians bring
 Their goods along the Western Road.

Yes, here, or hereabouts, they met
 To hold their racial talks and such—
To barter beads for Whitby jet,
 And tin for gay shell torques and such.

But long and long before that time
 (When bison used to roam on it)
Did Taffy and her Daddy climb
 That Down, and had their home on it.

Then beavers built in Broadstonebrook
 And made a swamp where Bramley stands;
And bears from Shere would come and look
 For Taffimai where Shamley stands.

MERROW DOWN

The Wey, that Taffy called Wagai,
 Was more than six times bigger then;
And all the Tribe of Tegumai
 They cut a noble figure then!

II

Of all the Tribe of Tegumai
 Who cut that figure, none remain,—
On Merrow Down the cuckoos cry—
 The silence and the sun remain.

But as the faithful years return
 And hearts unwounded sing again,
Comes Taffy dancing through the fern
 To lead the Surrey spring again.

Her brows are bound with bracken-fronds,
 And golden elf-locks fly above;
Her eyes are bright as diamonds
 And bluer than the sky above.

In mocassins and deer-skin cloak,
 Unfearing, free and fair she flits,
And lights her little damp-wood smoke
 To show her Daddy where she flits.

For far—oh, very far behind,
 So far she cannot call to him,
Comes Tegumai alone to find
 The daughter that was all to him.

THE LOOKING–GLASS

(A Country Dance)

QUEEN Bess was Harry's daughter.   Stand fo
 ward partners all!
  In ruff and stomacher and gown
She danced King Philip down-a down,
And left her shoe to show 'twas true—
  (The very tune I'm playing you)
In Norgem at Brickwall!

The Queen was in her chamber, and she was middling ol
Her petticoat was satin, and her stomacher was gold.
Backwards and forwards and sideways did she pass,
Making up her mind to face the cruel looking-glass.
  The cruel looking-glass that will never show a lass
  As comely or as kindly or as young as what she wa:

Queen Bess was Harry's daughter.   Now hand you
  partners all!

The Queen was in her chamber, a-combing of her hai
There came Queen Mary's spirit and It stood behin
  her chair,
Singing 'Backwards and forwards and sideways ma
  you pass,
But I will stand behind you till you face the looking-glas
  The cruel looking-glass that will never show a lass
  As lovely or unlucky or as lonely as I was!'

ueen Bess was Harry's daughter.   Now turn your
    partners all!

he Queen was in her chamber, a-weeping very sore.
here came Lord Leicester's spirit and It scratched upon
    the door,
nging 'Backwards and forwards and sideways may
    you pass,
ut I will walk beside you till you face the looking-glass.
 The cruel looking-glass that will never show a lass,
 As hard and unforgiving or as wicked as you was!'

ueen Bess was Harry's daughter.   Now kiss your
    partners all!

he Queen was in her chamber, her sins were on her
    head.
he looked the spirits up and down and statelily she
    said:—
Backwards and forwards and sideways though I've
    been,
et I am Harry's daughter and I am England's Queen!'
 And she faced the looking-glass (and whatever else
    there was),
 And she saw her day was over and she saw her beauty
    pass
 In the cruel looking-glass, that can always hurt a lass
 More hard than any ghost there is or any man there
    was!

THE QUEEN'S MEN

VALOUR and Innocence
  Have latterly gone hence
  To certain death by certain shame attended.
Envy—ah! even to tears!—
The fortune of their years
Which, though so few, yet so divinely ended.

Scarce had they lifted up
Life's full and fiery cup,
Than they had set it down untouched before them.
Before their day arose
They beckoned it to close—
Close in confusion and destruction o'er them.

They did not stay to ask
What prize should crown their task,
Well sure that prize was such as no man strives for;
But passed into eclipse,
Her kiss upon their lips—
Even Belphœbe's, whom they gave their lives for!

THE BELLS AND THE QUEEN, 1911

G AY go up and gay go down
    To ring the Bells of London Town.'
    When London Town's asleep in bed
'ou'll hear the Bells ring overhead,
    In excelsis gloria!
    Ringing for Victoria,
.inging for their mighty mistress—ten years dead!

[H]ere is more gain than Gloriana guessed,
    Than Gloriana guessed or Indies bring—
'han golden Indies bring.   A Queen confessed,
    A Queen confessed that crowned her people King.
[H]er people King, and crowned all Kings above,
    Above all Kings have crowned their Queen their
        love—
[H]ave crowned their love their Queen, their Queen their
        love!

[D]enying her, we do ourselves deny,
    Disowning her are we ourselves disowned.
[M]irror was she of our fidelity,
    And handmaid of our destiny enthroned;
[T]he very marrow of Youth's dream, and still
[Y]oke-mate of wisest Age that worked her will!

177

Our fathers had declared to us her praise.
　Her praise the years had proven past all speech,
And past all speech our loyal hearts always,
　Always our hearts lay open, each to each;
Therefore men gave their treasure and their blood
To this one woman—for she understood!

Four o' the clock!　Now all the world is still.
Oh, London Bells, to all the world declare
The Secret of the Empire—read who will!
The Glory of the People—touch who dare!

The Bells:
　　Power that has reached itself all kingly powers,
　　　　St. Margaret's:　By love o'erpowered—
　　　　St. Martin's:　By love o'erpowered—
　　　　St. Clement Danes:　By love o'erpowered,
　　　　　　　　The greater power confers!

The Bells:
　　For we were hers, as she, as she was ours,
　　　　Bow Bells:　And she was ours—
　　　　St. Paul's:　And she was ours—
　　　　Westminster:　And she was ours,
　　　　　　　　As we, even we, were hers!

The Bells:
　　As we were hers!

THE CITY OF SLEEP

OVER the edge of the purple down,
    Where the single lamplight gleams,
    Know ye the road to the Merciful Town
    That is hard by the Sea of Dreams—
Where the poor may lay their wrongs away,
    And the sick may forget to weep?
But we—pity us! Oh, pity us!
    We wakeful; ah, pity us!—
We must go back with Policeman Day—
    Back from the City of Sleep!

Weary they turn from the scroll and crown,
    Fetter and prayer and plough—
They that go up to the Merciful Town,
    For her gates are closing now.
It is their right in the Baths of Night
    Body and soul to steep,
But we—pity us! ah, pity us!
    We wakeful; oh, pity us!—
We must go back with Policeman Day—
    Back from the City of Sleep!

Over the edge of the purple down,
    Ere the tender dreams begin,
Look—we may look—at the Merciful Town,
    But we may not enter in!

179

Outcasts all, from her guarded wall
   Back to our watch we creep:
We—pity us! ah, pity us!
   We wakeful; oh, pity us!—
We that go back with Policeman Day—
   Back from the City of Sleep!

THE WIDOWER

FOR a season there must be pain—
   For a little, little space
   I shall lose the sight of her face,
Take back the old life again
While She is at rest in her place.

For a season this pain must endure,
   For a little, little while
I shall sigh more often than smile
Till Time shall work me a cure,
   And the pitiful days beguile.

For that season we must be apart,
   For a little length of years,
Till my life's last hour nears,
And, above the beat of my heart,
   I hear Her voice in my ears.

But I shall not understand—
   Being set on some later love,
Shall not know her for whom I strove,
Till she reach me forth her hand
Saying 'Who but I have the right?'
   And out of a troubled night
Shall draw me safe to the land.

CHAPTER HEADINGS

Just So Stories

WHEN the cabin port-holes are dark and green
    Because of the seas outside;
    When the ship goes wop (with a wiggle between)
And the steward falls into the soup-tureen,
    And the trunks begin to slide;
When Nursey lies on the floor in a heap,
And Mummy tells you to let her sleep,
And you aren't waked or washed or dressed,
Why, then you will know (if you haven't guessed)
You're 'Fifty North and Forty West!'
                'How the Whale got his Throat.'

The Camel's hump is an ugly lump
    Which well you may see at the Zoo;
But uglier yet is the hump we get
    From having too little to do.

Kiddies and grown-ups too-oo-oo,
If we haven't enough to do-oo-oo,
      We get the hump—
      Cameelious hump—
The hump that is black and blue!

We climb out of bed with a frouzly head
    And a snarly-yarly voice.

We shiver and scowl and we grunt and we growl
  At our bath and our boots and our toys;

And there ought to be a corner for me
(And I know there is one for you)
    When we get the hump—
    Cameelious hump—
The hump that is black and blue!

The cure for this ill is not to sit still,
  Or frowst with a book by the fire;
But to take a large hoe and a shovel also,
  And dig till you gently perspire;

And then you will find that the sun and the wind,
And the Djinn of the Garden too,
    Have lifted the hump—
    The horrible hump—
The hump that is black and blue!

I get it as well as you-oo-oo—
If I haven't enough to do-oo-oo!
    We all get hump—
    Cameelious hump—
Kiddies and grown-ups too!
             'How the Camel got his Hump.'

I am the Most Wise Baviaan, saying in most wise tones,
'Let us melt into the landscape—just us two by our
  lones.'
People have come—in a carriage—calling. But Mum-
  my is there. . . .
Yes, I can go if you take me—Nurse says she don't care.

183

Let's go up to the pig-styes and sit on the farmyard rails!
Let's say things to the bunnies, and watch 'em skitte
    their tails!
Let's—oh, anything, daddy, so long as it's you and me
And going truly exploring, and not being in till tea!
Here's your boots (I've brought 'em), and here's you
    cap and stick,
And here's your pipe and tobacco.   Oh, come along ou
    of it—quick!

                'How the Leopard got his Spots.'

I keep six honest serving-men
  (They taught me all I knew);
Their names are What and Why and When
  And How and Where and Who.
I send them over land and sea,
  I send them east and west;
But after they have worked for me,
  I give them all a rest.

I let them rest from nine till five,
  For I am busy then,
As well as breakfast, lunch, and tea,
  For they are hungry men.
But different folk have different views;
  I know a person small—
She keeps ten million serving-men,
  Who get no rest at all!
She sends 'em abroad on her own affairs,
  From the second she opens her eyes—
One million Hows, two million Wheres,
  And seven million Whys!

                'The Elephant's Child.'

This is the mouth-filling song of the race that was run
by a Boomer.
Run in a single burst—only event of its kind—
Started by Big God Nqong from Warrigaborrigarooma,
Old Man Kangaroo first, Yellow-Dog Dingo behind.

Kangaroo bounded away, his back-legs working like
pistons—
Bounded from morning till dark, twenty-five feet at a
bound.
Yellow-Dog Dingo lay like a yellow cloud in the distance—
Much too busy to bark. My! but they covered the
ground!

Nobody knows where they went, or followed the track
that they flew in,
For that Continent hadn't been given a name.
They ran thirty degrees, from Torres Straits to the
Leeuwin
(Look at the Atlas, please), then they ran back as they
came.

S'posing you could trot from Adelaide to the Pacific,
For an afternoon's run—half what these gentlemen did—
You would feel rather hot, but your legs would develop
terrific—
Yes, my importunate son, you'd be a Marvellous Kid!
'The Sing-Song of Old Man Kangaroo.'

I've never sailed the Amazon,
   I've never reached Brazil;
But the 'Don' and 'Magdalena,'
   They can go there when they will!

Yes, weekly from Southampton,
Great steamers, white and gold,
Go rolling down to Rio
(Roll down—roll down to Rio!)
And I'd like to roll to Rio
Some day before I'm old!

I've never seen a Jaguar,
　Nor yet an Armadill—
O dilloing in his armour,
　And I s'pose I never will,

Unless I go to Rio
These wonders to behold—
Roll down—roll down to Rio—
Roll really down to Rio!
Oh, I'd love to roll to Rio
Some day before I'm old!
'The Beginning of the Armadilloes.'

China-going P. and O.'s
Pass Pau Amma's playground close,
And his Pusat Tasek lies
Near the track of most B. I.'s.
N. Y. K. and N. D. L.
Know Pau Amma's home as well
As the Fisher of the Sea knows
'Bens,' M. M.'s, and Rubattinos.
But (and this is rather queer)
A. T. L.'s can not come here;
O. and O. and D. O. A.
Must go round another way.
Orient, Anchor, Bibby, Hall,
Never go that way at all.

U. C. S would have a fit
If it found itself on it.
And if 'Beavers' took their cargoes
To Penang instead of Lagos,
Or a fat Shaw-Savill bore
Passengers to Singapore,
Or a White Star were to try a
Little trip to Sourabaya,
Or a B. S. A. went on
Past Natal to Cheribon,
Then great Mr. Lloyds would come
With a wire and drag them home!

. . . . . .

You'll know what my riddle means
When you've eaten mangosteens.
                    'The Crab that Played with the Sea.'

Pussy can sit by the fire and sing,
    Pussy can climb a tree,
Or play with a silly old cork and string
    To 'muse herself, not me.
But I like Binkie my dog, because
    He knows how to behave;
So, Binkie's the same as the First Friend was,
    And I am the Man in the Cave!

Pussy will play man-Friday till
    It's time to wet her paw
And make her walk on the window-sill
    (For the footprint Crusoe saw);

Then she fluffles her tail and mews,
 And scratches and won't attend.
But Binkie will play whatever I choose,
 And he is my true First Friend!

Pussy will rub my knees with her head
 Pretending she loves me hard;
But the very minute I go to my bed
 Pussy runs out in the yard,
And there she stays till the morning-light;
 So I know it is only pretend;
But Binkie, he snores at my feet all night,
 And he is my Firstest Friend!
          'The Cat that Walked by Himself.'

There was never a Queen like Balkis,
 From here to the wide world's end;
But Balkis talked to a butterfly
 As you would talk to a friend.

There was never a King like Solomon,
 Not since the world began;
But Solomon talked to a butterfly
 As a man would talk to a man.

She was Queen of Sabæa—
 And he was Asia's Lord—
But they both of 'em talked to butterflies
 When they took their walks abroad!
          'The Butterfly that Stamped.'

THE PRAYER OF MIRIAM COHEN

FROM the wheel and the drift of Things
    Deliver us, Good Lord,
And we will face the wrath of Kings,
    The faggot and the sword!

Lay not Thy Works before our eyes,
    Nor vex us with Thy Wars,
Lest we should feel the straining skies
    O'ertrod by trampling stars.

Hold us secure behind the gates
    Of saving flesh and bone,
Lest we should dream what dream awaits
    The soul escaped alone.

Thy Path, Thy Purposes conceal
    From our beleaguered realm,
Lest any shattering whisper steal
    Upon us and o'erwhelm.

A veil 'twixt us and Thee, Good Lord,
    A veil 'twixt us and Thee,
Lest we should hear too clear, too clear,
    And unto madness see!

THE SONG OF THE LITTLE HUNTER

ERE Mor the Peacock flutters, ere the Monkey
    People cry,
    Ere Chil the Kite swoops down a furlong sheer,
Through the Jungle very softly flits a shadow and a
    sigh—
    He is Fear, O Little Hunter, he is Fear!
Very softly down the glade runs a waiting, watching
    shade,
    And the whisper spreads and widens far and near.
And the sweat is on thy brow, for he passes even now—
    He is Fear, O Little Hunter, he is Fear!

Ere the moon has climbed the mountain, ere the rocks
    are ribbed with light,
    When the downward-dipping trails are dank and
    drear,
Comes a breathing hard behind thee—snuffle-snuffle
    through the night—
    It is Fear, O Little Hunter, it is Fear!
On thy knees and draw the bow; bid the shrilling arrow
    go;
    In the empty, mocking thicket plunge the spear!
But thy hands are loosed and weak, and the blood has
    left thy cheek—
    It is Fear, O Little Hunter, it is Fear!

THE SONG OF THE LITTLE HUNTER

When the heat-cloud sucks the tempest, when the
    slivered pine-trees fall,
  When the blinding, blaring rain-squalls lash and veer,
Through the war-gongs of the thunder rings a voice
    more loud than all—
  It is Fear, O Little Hunter, it is Fear!
Now the spates are banked and deep; now the footless
    boulders leap—
  Now the lightning shows each littlest leaf-rib clear—
But thy throat is shut and dried, and thy heart against
    thy side
  Hammers: Fear, O Little Hunter—this is Fear!

GOW'S WATCH

Act II.   Scene 2.

The pavilion in the Gardens.   Enter Ferdinand and the
King.

FERDINAND.   Your tiercel's too long at hack,
     Sir.   He's no eyass
     But a passage-hawk that footed ere we caught him,
Dangerously free o' the air.   Faith were he mine
(As mine's the glove he binds to for his tirings)
I'd fly him with a make-hawk.   He's in yarak
Plumed to the very point.   So manned so weathered!
Give him the firmament God made him for
And what shall take the air of him?

   The King.   A young wing yet
Bold—overbold on the perch, but think you, Ferdinand,
He can endure the tall skies yonder?   Cozen
Advantage out of the teeth of the hurricane?
Choose his own mate against the lammer-geier?
Ride out a night-long tempest, hold his pitch
Between the lightning and the cloud it leaps from,
Never too pressed to kill?

   Ferdinand.   I'll answer for him.
Bating all parable, I know the Prince.
There's a bleak devil in the young, my Lord,

God put it there to save 'em from their elders
And break their father's heart, but bear them scatheless
Through mire and thorns and blood if need be.   Think
What our prime saw! Such glory, such achievements
As now our children wondering at, examine
Themselves to see if they shall hardly equal.
But what cared we while we wrought the wonders?
    Nothing!
The rampant deed contented.

    The King.   Little enough, God knows! But after-
       wards?   After—
There comes the reckoning. I would save him that.

    Ferdinand.   Save him dry scars that ache of winter-
       nights,
Worn out self-pity and as much of knowledge
As makes old men fear judgment?   Then loose him—
       loose him—
A' God's name loose him to adventure early!
And trust some random pike, or half-backed horse,
Besides what's caught in Italy, to save him.

    The King. I know. I know. And yet. . . .
       What stirs in the garden?

Enter Gow and a Gardener bearing the Prince's body.

    Ferdinand.   (Gods give me patience!) Gow and a
       gardener
Bearing some load along in the dusk to the dunghill.
Nay—a dead branch— But as I said, the Prince—

    The King. They've set it down. Strange they
      should work so late.

Gow (setting down the body).   Heark, you unsanctified fool while I set out our story.   We found it, this side the North Park wall which it had climbed to pluck nectarines from the alley.   Heark again!   There was a nectarine in its hand when we found it, and the naughty brick that slipped from the coping beneath its foot and so caused its death, lies now under the wall for the King to see.

The King (above).   The King to see!   Why should he?   Who's the man?

Gow.   That is your tale.   Swerve from it by so much as the breadth of my dagger and here's your instant reward.   You heard not, saw not, and by the Horns of ninefold-cuckolded Jupiter you thought not nor dreamed not anything more or other!

The King.   Ninefold-cuckolded Jupiter.   That's a rare oath!   Shall we look closer?

Ferdinand.   Not yet, my Lord!   (I cannot hear him breathe.)

Gardener.   The North Park wall?   It was so.   Plucking nectarines.   It shall be.   But how shall I say if any ask why our Lady the Queen—

Gow (stabs him).   Thus!   Hie after the Prince and tell him y'are the first fruits of his nectarine tree.   Bleed there behind the laurels.

The King.   Why did Gow buffet the clown?   What said he?   I'll go look.

Ferdinand (above).   Save yourself!   It is the King!

Enter the King and Ferdinand to Gow.

194

Gow. God save you! This was the Prince!

The King. The Prince! Not a dead branch? (Uncovers the face.) My flesh and blood! My son! my son! my son!

Ferdinand (to Gow). I had feared something of this. And that fool yonder?

Gow. Dead, or as good. He cannot speak.

Ferdinand. Better so.

The King. 'Loosed to adventure early!' Tell the tale.

Gow. Saddest truth alack! I came upon him not a half hour since, fallen from the North Park wall over against the Deer-park side—dead—dead!—a nectarine in his hand that the dear lad must have climbed for, and plucked the very instant, look you, that a brick slipped on the coping. 'Tis there now. So I lifted him, but his neck was as you see—and already cold.

The King. Oh, very cold. But why should he have troubled to climb? He was free of all the fruit in my garden, God knows! . . . What, Gow?

Gow. Surely, God knows!

The King. A lad's trick. But I love him the better for it. . . . True, he's past loving. . . . And now we must tell our Queen. What a coil at the day's end! She'll grieve for him. Not as I shall, Ferdinand, but as youth for youth. They were much of the same age. Playmate for playmate. See, he wears her colours. That is the knot she gave him last—last . . . Oh God! When was yesterday?

Ferdinand. Come in! Come in, my Lord. There's a dew falling.

The King. He'll take no harm of it. I'll follow
    presently. . . .
He's all his mother's now and none of mine—
Her very face on the bride-pillow. Yet I tricked her.
But that was later—and she never guessed.
I do not think he sinned much—he's too young—
Much the same age as my Queen. God must not judge
    him
Too hardly for such slips as youth may fall in.
But I'll entreat that Throne.
    (Prays by the body.)

Gow. The Heavens hold up still. Earth opens not
and this dew's mere water. What shall a man think of
it all? (To Gardener.) Not dead yet, sirrah? I bade
you follow the Prince. Despatch!

Gardener. Some kind soul pluck out the dagger.
Why did you slay me? I'd done no wrong. I'd ha'
kept it secret till my dying day. But not now—not
now! I'm dying. The Prince fell from the Queen's
chamber window. I saw it in the nut alley. He was—

Ferdinand. But what made you in the nut alley at
that hour?

Gardener. No wrong. No more than another man's
wife. Jocasta of the still-room. She'd kissed me good-
night too; but that's over with the rest. . . . I've
stumbled on the Prince's beastly loves, and I pay for all.
Let me pass!

Gow. Count it your fortune, honest man. You
would have revealed it to your woman at the next meeting. You flesh-mongers are all one feather. (Plucks
out the dagger.)

Go in peace and lay your death to Fortune's door.
He's sped—thank Fortune!

Ferdinand. Who knows not Fortune, glutted on
    easy thrones,
Stealing from feasts as rare to coney-catch
Privily in the hedgerows for a clown,
With that same cruel-lustful hand and eye,
Those nails and wedges, that one hammer and lead,
And the very gerb of long-stored lightning loosed
Yesterday 'gainst some King.

The King. I have pursued with prayers where my
    heart warns me
My soul shall overtake—

Enter the Queen.

The King. Look not! Wait till I tell you, dearest.
    . . . Air! . . .
'Loosed to adventure early'
. . . I go late. (Dies.)

Gow. So! God hath cut off the Prince in his pleas-
ures. Gow, to save the King, hath silenced one poor
fool who knew how it befell, and now the King's dead,
needs only that the Queen should kill Gow and all's safe
for her this side o' the Judgment. . . . Senor Ferdinand, the wind's easterly. I'm for the road.

Ferdinand. My horse is at the gate. God speed
you. Whither?

Gow. To the Duke, if the Queen does not lay hands
on me before. However it goes, I charge you bear witness, Senor Ferdinand, I served the old King faithfully.
To the death, Senor Ferdinand—to the death!

THE WISHING CAPS

L IFE'S all getting and giving.
   I've only myself to give.
   What shall I do for a living?
I've only one life to live.
End it? I'll not find another.
Spend it? But how shall I best?
Sure the wise plan is to live like a man,
And Luck may look after the rest!
   Largesse! Largesse, Fortune!
   Give or hold at your will.
   If I've no care for Fortune
   Fortune must follow me still.

Bad Luck, she is never a lady
But the commonest wench on the street,
Shuffling, shabby and shady,
Shameless to pass or meet.
Walk with her once—it's a weakness!
Talk to her twice—it's a crime!
Thrust her away when she gives you 'good day'
And the besom won't board you next time.
   Largesse! Largesse, Fortune!
   What is Your Ladyship's mood?
   If I've no care for Fortune,
   My Fortune is bound to be good!

THE WISHING CAPS

Good Luck she is never a lady
But the cursedest quean alive!
Tricksey, wincing and jady,
Kittle to lead or drive.
Greet her—she's hailing a stranger!
Meet her—she's busking to leave.
Let her alone for a shrew to the bone,
And the hussy comes plucking your sleeve!
  Largesse! Largesse, Fortune!
  I'll neither follow nor flee.
  If I don't run after Fortune
  Fortune must run after me!

'BY THE HOOF OF THE WILD GOAT'

BY the Hoof of the Wild Goat uptossed
    From the cliff where she lay in the Sun,
    Fell the Stone
To the Tarn where the daylight is lost;
So she fell from the light of the Sun,
        And alone!

Now the fall was ordained from the first,
With the Goat and the Cliff and the Tarn,
      But the Stone
Knows only her life is accursed,
As she sinks from the light of the Sun,
        And alone!

Oh Thou Who hast builded the World!
Oh Thou Who hast lighted the Sun!
Oh Thou Who hast darkened the Tarn!
      Judge Thou
The sin of the Stone that was hurled
By the goat from the light of the Sun,
As she sinks in the mire of the Tarn,
      Even now—even now—even now!

THE DAWN WIND

AT two o'clock in the morning, if you open your
window and listen,
You will hear the feet of the Wind that is going
to call the sun.
And the trees in the shadow rustle and the trees in the
moonlight glisten,
And though it is deep, dark night, you feel that the
night is done.

So do the cows in the field.   They graze for an hour and
lie down,
Dozing and chewing the cud; or a bird in the ivy
wakes,
Chirrups one note and is still, and the restless Wind
strays on,
Fidgeting far down the road, till, softly, the darkness
breaks.

Back comes the Wind full strength with a blow like an
angel's wing,
Gentle but waking the world, as he shouts: 'The Sun!
The Sun!'
And the light floods over the fields and the birds begin to
sing,
And the Wind dies down in the grass.   It is Day and
his work is done.

So when the world is asleep, and there seems no hope of
her waking
Out of some long, bad dream that makes her mutter
and moan,
Suddenly, all men arise to the noise of fetters breaking,
And every one smiles at his neighbour and tells him
his soul is his own!

SONG OF THE RED WAR–BOAT

(A. D. 683)

SHOVE off from the wharf-edge! Steady!
    Watch for a smooth! Give way!
    If she feels the lop already
      She'll stand on her head in the bay.
It's ebb—it's dusk—it's blowing,
    The shoals are a mile of white,
But (snatch her along!) we're going
    To find our master to-night.

    For we hold that in all disaster
      Of shipwreck, storm, or sword,
    A Man must stand by his Master
      When once he has pledged his word.

Raging seas have we rowed in,
    But we seldom saw them thus,
Our master is angry with Odin—
    Odin is angry with us!
Heavy odds have we taken,
    But never before such odds.
The Gods know they are forsaken,
    We must risk the wrath of the Gods!

Over the crest she flies from,
   Into its hollow she drops,
Cringes and clears her eyes from
   The wind-torn breaker-tops,
Ere out on the shrieking shoulder
   Of a hill-high surge she drives.
Meet her! Meet her and hold her!
   Pull for your scoundrel lives!

The thunders bellow and clamour
   The harm that they mean to do!
There goes Thor's own Hammer
   Cracking the dark in two!
Close! But the blow has missed her,
   Here comes the wind of the blow!
Row or the squall'll twist her
   Broadside on to it!—Row!

Heark 'ee, Thor of the Thunder,
   We are not here for a jest—
For wager, warfare or plunder,
   Or to put your power to test.
This work is none of our wishing—
   We would house at home if we might—
But our master is wrecked out fishing.
   We go to find him to-night.

For we hold that in all disaster—
   As the Gods Themselves have said—
A Man must stand by his Master
   Till one of the two is dead.

SONG OF THE RED WAR-BOAT

That is our way of thinking,
  Now you can do as you will.
While we try to save her from sinking
  And hold her head to it still.
Bale her and keep her moving,
  Or she'll break her back in the trough. . . .
Who said the weather's improving,
  Or the swells are taking off?

Sodden, and chafed and aching,
  Gone in the loins and knees—
No matter—the day is breaking,
  And there's far less weight to the seas!
Up mast, and finish baling—
  In oars, and out with the mead—
The rest will be two-reef sailing. . . .
  That was a night indeed!

  But we hold that in all disaster
    (And faith, we have found it true!)
  If only you stand by your master,
    The Gods will stand by you!

HUNTING–SONG OF THE SEEONEE PACK

AS the dawn was breaking the Sambhur belled—
Once, twice and again!
And a doe leaped up, and a doe leaped up
From the pond in the wood where the wild deer sup.
This I, scouting alone, beheld,
Once, twice and again!

As the dawn was breaking the Sambhur belled—
Once, twice and again!
And a wolf stole back, and a wolf stole back
To carry the word to the waiting pack,
And we sought and we found and we bayed on his track
Once, twice and again!

As the dawn was breaking the Wolf Pack yelled
Once, twice and again!
Feet in the jungle that leave no mark!
Eyes that can see in the dark—the dark!
Tongue—give tongue to it! Hark! O hark!
Once, twice and again!

BLUE ROSES

ROSES red and roses white
  Plucked I for my love's delight.
  She would none of all my posies—
Bade me gather her blue roses.

Half the world I wandered through,
Seeking where such flowers grew.
Half the world unto my quest
Answered me with laugh and jest.

Home I came at wintertide,
But my silly love had died,
Seeking with her latest breath
Roses from the arms of Death.

It may be beyond the grave
She shall find what she would have.
Mine was but an idle quest—
Roses white and red are best.

A RIPPLE SONG

O NCE a ripple came to land
    In the golden sunset burning—
    Lapped against a maiden's hand,
    By the ford returning.

Dainty foot and gentle breast—
Here, across, be glad and rest.
'Maiden, wait,' the ripple saith;
'Wait awhile, for I am Death!'

'Where my lover calls I go—
    Shame it were to treat him coldly—
'Twas a fish that circled so,
    Turning over boldly.'

Dainty foot and tender heart,
Wait the loaded ferry-cart.
'Wait, ah, wait!' the ripple saith;
'Maiden, wait, for I am Death!'

'When my lover calls I haste—
    Dame Disdain was never wedded!'
Ripple-ripple round her waist,
    Clear the current eddied.

A RIPPLE SONG

Foolish heart and faithful hand,
Little feet that touched no land.
Far away the ripple sped,
Ripple—ripple—running red!

PSYCHE AND THE CHILDREN

EYES aloft, over dangerous places,
  The children follow where Psyche flies,
  And, in the sweat of their upturned faces,
  Slash with a net at the empty skies.

So it goes they fall amid brambles,
  And sting their toes on the nettle-tops,
Till after a thousand scratches and scrambles,
  They wipe their brows and the hunting stops.

Then to quiet them comes their father
  And stills the riot of pain and grief,
Saying, 'Little ones, go and gather
  Out of my garden a cabbage-leaf.

'You will find on it whorls and clots of
  Dull gray eggs that, properly fed,
Turn, by way of the worm, to lots of
  Radiant Psyches raised from the dead.'

.   .   .   .   .

'Heaven is beautiful, Earth is ugly,'
  The three-dimensioned preacher saith,
So we must not look where the snail and the slug lie
  For Psyche's birth. . . . And that is our death

210

MY LADY'S LAW

THE Law whereby my lady moves
    Was never Law to me,
But 'tis enough that she approves,
    Whatever Law it be.

For in that Law, and by that Law,
    My constant course I'll steer;
Not that I heed or deem it dread,
    But that she holds it dear.

Tho' Asia sent for my content
    Her richest argosies,
Those would I spurn, and bid return,
    If that should give her ease.

With equal heart I'd watch depart
    Each spiced sail from sight,
Sans bitterness, desiring less
    Great gear than her delight.

Though Kings made swift with many a gift
    My proven sword to hire—
I would not go nor serve 'em so—
    Except at her desire.

With even mind, I'd put behind
　　Adventure and acclaim,
And clean give o'er, esteeming more
　　Her favour than my fame.

Yet such am I, yea such am I—
　　Sore bond and freest free,
The Law that sways my lady's ways
　　Is mystery to me!

SONGS FROM BOOKS

Our sister sayeth such and such,
And we must bow to her behests;
Our sister toileth overmuch,
Our little maid that hath no breasts.

THE NURSING SISTER

(Maternity Hospital)

OUR sister sayeth such and such,
　　And we must bow to her behests;
Our sister toileth overmuch,
　　Our little maid that hath no breasts.

A field untilled, a web unwove,
　　A flower withheld from sun or bee,
An alien in the courts of Love,
　　And—teacher unto such as we!

We love her, but we laugh the while,
　　We laugh, but sobs are mixed with laughter;
Our sister hath no time to smile,
　　She knows not what must follow after.

Wind of the South, arise and blow,
　　From beds of spice thy locks shake free;
Breathe on her heart that she may know,
　　Breathe on her eyes that she may see.

Alas! we vex her with our mirth,
　　And maze her with most tender scorn,
Who stands beside the gates of Birth,
　　Herself a child—a child unborn!

213

Our sister sayeth such and such,
   And we must bow to her behests;
Our sister toileth overmuch,
   Our little maid that hath no breasts.

THE LOVE SONG OF HAR DYAL

ALONE upon the housetops to the North
    I turn and watch the lightning in the sky,—
The glamour of thy footsteps in the North.
    Come back to me, Beloved, or I die.

Below my feet the still bazar is laid—
    Far, far below the weary camels lie—
The camels and the captives of thy raid.
    Come back to me, Beloved, or I die!

My father's wife is old and harsh with years,
    And drudge of all my father's house am I—
My bread is sorrow and my drink is tears.
    Come back to me, Beloved, or I die!

A DEDICATION

AND they were stronger hands than mine
    That digged the Ruby from the earth—
    More cunning brains that made it worth
The large desire of a king,
And stouter hearts that through the brine
Went down the perfect Pearl to bring.

Lo, I have wrought in common clay
Rude figures of a rough-hewn race,
Since pearls strew not the market-place
In this my town of banishment,
Where with the shifting dust I play,
And eat the bread of discontent.

Yet is there life in that I make.
O thou who knowest, turn and see—
As thou hast power over me
So have I power over these
Because I wrought them for thy sake,
And breathed in them mine agonies.

Small mirth was in the making—now
I lift the cloth that cloaks the clay,
And, wearied, at thy feet I lay
My wares, ere I go forth to sell.
The long bazar will praise, but thou—
Heart of my heart—have I done well?

MOTHER O' MINE

IF I were hanged on the highest hill,
　　Mother o' mine, O mother o' mine!
I know whose love would follow me still,
　　Mother o' mine, O mother o' mine!

If I were drowned in the deepest sea,
　　Mother o' mine, O mother o' mine!
I know whose tears would come down to me,
　　Mother o' mine, O mother o' mine!

If I were damned of body and soul,
I know whose prayers would make me whole,
　　Mother o' mine, O mother o' mine!

THE ONLY SON

SHE dropped the bar, she shot the bolt, she fed the
   fire anew,
   For she heard a whimper under the sill and a great
     gray paw came through.
The fresh flame comforted the hut and shone on the roof-
   beam,
And the Only Son lay down again and dreamed that he
   dreamed a dream.
The last ash fell from the withered log with the click of a
   falling spark,
And the Only Son woke up again, and called across the
   dark:—
'Now was I born of womankind and laid in a mother's
   breast?
For I have dreamed of a shaggy hide whereon I went to
   rest?
And was I born of womankind and laid on a father's
   arm?
For I have dreamed of clashing teeth that guarded me
   from harm.
And was I born an Only Son and did I play alone?
For I have dreamed of comrades twain that bit me to
   the bone.
And did I break the barley-cake and steep it in the tyre?
For I have dreamed of a youngling kid new-riven from
   the byre.

'or I have dreamed of a midnight sky and a midnight
  call to blood
ۛnd red-mouthed shadows racing by, that thrust me
  from my food.
Tis an hour yet and an hour yet to the rising of the
  moon,
ۛut I can see the black roof-tree as plain as it were noon.
Tis a league and a league to the Lena Falls where the
  trooping blackbuck go;
ۛut I can hear the little fawn that bleats behind the doe.
Tis a league and a league to the Lena Falls where the
  crop and the upland meet,
ۛut I can smell the wet dawn-wind that wakes the
  sprouting wheat.
ۛnbar the door, I may not bide, but I must out and see
ۛf those are wolves that wait outside or my own kin to
  me!'

.   .   .   .

ۛhe loosed the bar, she slid the bolt, she opened the door
  anon,
ۛnd a gray bitch-wolf came out of the dark and fawned
  on the Only Son!

MOWGLI'S SONG AGAINST PEOPLE

I WILL let loose against you the fleet-footed vines—
I will call in the Jungle to stamp out your lines!
    The roofs shall fade before it,
      The house-beams shall fall,
    And the Karela, the bitter Karela,
      Shall cover it all!

In the gates of these your councils my people shall sing,
In the doors of these your garners the Bat-folk shall
    cling;
    And the snake shall be your watchman,
      By a hearthstone unswept;
    For the Karela, the bitter Karela,
      Shall fruit where ye slept!

Ye shall not see my strikers; ye shall hear them and
    guess;
By night, before the moon-rise, I will send for my cess,
    And the wolf shall be your herdsman
      By a landmark removed,
    For the Karela, the bitter Karela,
      Shall seed where ye loved!

I will reap your fields before you at the hands of a host;
Ye shall glean behind my reapers for the bread that is lost;
    And the deer shall be your oxen

MOWGLI'S SONG AGAINST PEOPLE

On a headland untilled,
For the Karela, the bitter Karela,
Shall leaf where ye build!

have untied against you the club-footed vines—
have sent in the Jungle to swamp out your lines!
The trees—the trees are on you!
The house-beams shall fall,
And the Karela, the bitter Karela,
Shall cover you all!

ROMULUS AND REMUS

O	H, little did the Wolf-Child care—
	When first he planned his home,
What city should arise and bear
	The weight and state of Rome.

A shiftless, westward-wandering tramp,
	Checked by the Tiber flood,
He reared a wall around his camp
	Of uninspired mud.

But when his brother leaped the Wall
	And mocked its height and make,
He guessed the future of it all
	And slew him for its sake.

Swift was the blow—swift as the thought
	Which showed him in that hour
How unbelief may bring to naught
	The early steps of Power.

Foreseeing Time's imperilled hopes
	Of Glory, Grace, and Love—
All singers, Cæsars, artists, Popes—
	Would fail if Remus throve.

ROMULUS AND REMUS

He sent his brother to the Gods,
    And, when the fit was o'er,
Went on collecting turves and clods
    To build the Wall once more!

THE EGG–SHELL

T HE wind took off with the sunset—
   The fog came up with the tide,
  When the Witch of the North took an Egg-she
   With a little Blue Devil inside.
'Sink,' she said, 'or swim,' she said,
   'It's all you will get from me.
And that is the finish of him!' she said,
   And the Egg-shell went to sea.

The wind fell dead with the midnight—
   The fog shut down like a sheet,
When the Witch of the North heard the Egg-shell
   Feeling by hand for a fleet.
'Get!' she said, 'or you're gone,' she said,
   But the little Blue Devil said 'No!'
'The sights are just coming on,' he said,
   And he let the Whitehead go.

The wind got up with the morning—
   And the fog blew off with the rain,
When the Witch of the North saw the Egg-shell
   And the little Blue Devil again.
'Did you swim?' she said. 'Did you sink?' she said
   And the Little Blue Devil replied:
'For myself I swam, but I think,' he said.
   'There's somebody sinking outside.'

THE KING AND THE CHILDREN

ONCE on a time was a King anxious to understand
What was the wisest thing a man could do for
his land.

Most of his population hurried to answer the question,
each with a long oration, each with a new suggestion.
They interrupted his meals, he wasn't safe in his bed
from 'em,
They hung round his neck and heels, and at last His
Majesty fled from 'em.

He put on a leper's cloak (people leave lepers alone),
Out of the window he broke, and abdicated his throne.
All that rapturous day, while his Court and his Minis-
ters mourned him,
He danced on his own highway till his own Policemen
warned him.

Gay and cheerful he ran (lepers don't cheer as a rule)
Till he found a philosopher-man teaching an infant
school.

The windows were open wide, the King sat down on the
grass,
And heard the children inside reciting 'Our King is an
Ass.'

225

The King popped in his head 'Some people would ca
this treason,
But I think you are right,' he said; 'will you kindly giv
me your reason?'
Lepers in school are as rare as kings with a leper's dres
on,
But the class didn't stop or stare; it calmly went o
with the lesson:

'The wisest thing, we suppose, that a man can do for hi
land,
Is the work that lies under his nose, with the tools tha
lie under his hand.'
The King whipped off his cloak, and stood in his crow
before 'em.
He said:—'My dear little folk, "Ex ore parvulorum"
(Which is Latin for "Children know more than grown
ups would credit")
You have shown me the road to go, and I propose t
tread it.'

Back to his Kingdom he ran, and issued a Proclamatior
'Let every living man return to his occupation!'
Then he explained to the mob that cheered in his palac
and round it,
'I've been to look for a job, and Heaven be praised I'v
found it!'

THE KING'S TASK

AFTER the sack of the City, when Rome was sunk
to a name,
    In the years that the lights were darkened, or
ever St. Wilfrid came,
Low on the borders of Britain (the ancient poets sing)
Between the Cliff and the Forest there ruled a Saxon
King.
Stubborn all were his people from cottar to overlord—
Not to be cowed by the cudgel, scarce to be schooled by
the sword;
Quick to turn at their pleasure, cruel to cross in their
mood,
And set on paths of their choosing as the hogs of An-
dred's Wood.
Laws they made in the Witan—the laws of flaying and
fine—
Common, loppage and pannage, the theft and the track
of kine—
Statutes of tun and market for the fish and the malt and
the meal—
The tax on the Bramber packhorse and the tax on the
Hastings keel.
Over the graves of the Druids and under the wreck of
Rome,
Rudely but surely they bedded the plinth of the days to
come.

227

Behind the feet of the Legions and before the Norseman's ire,

Rudely but greatly begat they the framing of state and shire.

Rudely but deeply they laboured, and their labour stands till now,

If we trace on our ancient headlands the twist of their eight-ox plough.

There came a king from Hamtun, by Bosenham he came,

He filled Use with slaughter, and Lewes he gave to flame.

He smote while they sat in the Witan—sudden he smote and sore,

That his fleet was gathered at Selsea ere they mustered at Cymen's Ore.

Blithe went the Saxons to battle, by down and wood and mere,

But thrice the acorns ripened ere the western mark was clear.

Thrice was the beechmast gathered and the Beltane fires burned

Thrice, and the beeves were salted thrice ere the host returned.

They drove that king from Hamtun, by Bosenham o'erthrown,

Out of Rugnor to Wilton they made his land their own.

Camps they builded at Gilling, at Basing and Alresford,

But wrath abode in the Saxons from cottar to overlord.

Wrath at the weary war-game, at the foe that snapped and ran

Wolf-wise feigning and flying, and wolf-wise snatching his man.

Wrath for their spears unready, their levies new to the
blades—

Shame for the helpless sieges and the scornful ambus-
cades.

At hearth and tavern and market, wherever the tale was
told,

Shame and wrath had the Saxons because of their boasts
of old.

And some would drink and deny it, and some would
pray and atone;

But the most part, after their anger, avouched that the
sin was their own.

Wherefore, girding together, up to the Witan they came,

And as they had shouldered their bucklers so did they
shoulder their blame.

For that was the wont of the Saxons (the ancient poets
sing),

And first they spoke in the Witan and then they spoke
to the King:

'Edward King of the Saxons, thou knowest from sire to
son,

One is the King and his People—in gain and ungain one.

Count we the gain together. With doubtings and spread
dismays

We have broken a foolish people—but after many days.

Count we the loss together. Warlocks hampered our
arms.

We were tricked as by magic. we were turned as by
charms.

We went down to the battle and the road was plain to
keep,

But our angry eyes were holden, and we struck as they
strike in sleep—

Men new shaken from slumber, sweating, with eyes
    a-stare,
Little blows uncertain dealt on the useless air.
Also a vision betrayed us and a lying tale made bold
That we looked to hold what we had not and to have
    what we did not hold:
That a shield should give us shelter—that a sword should
    give us power,
A shield snatched up at a venture and a hilt scarce han-
    dled an hour:
That being rich in the open, we should be strong in the
    close—
And the Gods would sell us a cunning for the day that
    we met our foes.
This was the work of wizards, but not with our foe they
    bide,
In our own camp we took them, and their names are
    Sloth and Pride.
Our pride was before the battle; our sloth ere we lifted
    spear,
But hid in the heart of the people as the fever hides in
    the mere,
Waiting only the war-game, the heat of the strife to
    rise
As the ague fumes round Oxeney when the rotting reed-
    bed dries.
But now we are purged of that fever—cleansed by the
    letting of blood,
Something leaner of body—something keener of mood.
And the men new-freed from the levies return to the
    fields again,
Matching a hundred battles, cottar and lord and
    thane,

And they talk aloud in the temples where the ancient
war-gods are.

They thumb and mock and belittle the holy harness of
war.

They jest at the sacred chariots, the robes and the gilded
staff—

These things fill them with laughter, they lean on their
spears and laugh.

The men grown old in the war-game, hither and thither
they range—

And scorn and laughter together are sire and dam of
change;

And change may be good or evil—but we know not
what it will bring.

Therefore our King must teach us. That is thy task,
O King!'

TOGETHER

WHEN Horse and Rider each can trust the
other everywhere,
It takes a fence and more than a fence to
pound that happy pair;
For the one will do what the other demands, although he
is beaten and blown,
And when it is done, they can live through a run that
neither could face alone.

When Crew and Captain understand each other to the
core,
It takes a gale and more than a gale to put their ship
ashore;
For the one will do what the other commands, although
they are chilled to the bone,
And both together can live through weather that neither
could face alone.

When King and People understand each other past a
doubt,
It takes a foe and more than a foe to knock that country
out;
For the one will do what the other one asks as soon as
the need is known,
And hand in hand they can make a stand which neither
could make alone!

TOGETHER

This wisdom had Elizabeth and all her subjects too,
For she was theirs and they were hers, as well the
   Spaniard knew;
For when his grim Armada came to conquer the Nation
   and Throne,
Why, back to back they met an attack that neither
   could face alone!

It is not wealth nor talk nor trade nor schools nor even
   the Vote,
Will save your land when the enemy's hand is tightening
   round your throat.
But a King and a People who thoroughly trust each
   other in all that is done
Can sleep on their bed without any dread—for the
   world will leave 'em alone!

CHAPTER HEADINGS

The Jungle Books

NOW Chil the Kite brings home the night
    That Mang the Bat sets free—
The herds are shut in byre and hut
    For loosed till dawn are we.
This is the hour of pride and power,
    Talon and tush and claw.
Oh hear the call!—Good hunting all
    That keep the Jungle Law!
                   'Mowgli's Brothers.'

His spots are the joy of the Leopard: his horns are the
    Buffalo's pride.
Be clean, for the strength of the hunter is known by the
    gloss of his hide.
If ye find that the bullock can toss you, or the heavy-
    browed Sambhur can gore;
Ye need not stop work to inform us.   We knew it ten
    seasons before.
Oppress not the cubs of the stranger, but hail them as
    Sister and Brother,
For though they are little and fubsy, it may be the Bear
    is their mother.
'There is none like to me!' says the Cub in the pride of
    his earliest kill;

But the Jungle is large and the Cub he is small. Let
him think and be still.

'Kaa's Hunting.'

The stream is shrunk—the pool is dry,
And we be comrades, thou and I;
With fevered jowl and dusty flank
Each jostling each along the bank;
And, by one drouthy fear made still,
Foregoing thought of quest or kill.
Now 'neath his dam the fawn may see,
The lean Pack-wolf as cowed as he,
And the tall buck, unflinching, note
The fangs that tore his father's throat.
The pools are shrunk—the streams are dry,
And we be playmates, thou and I,
Till yonder cloud—Good Hunting!—loose
The rain that breaks our Water Truce.

'How Fear Came.'

What of the hunting, hunter bold?
Brother, the watch was long and cold.
What of the quarry ye went to kill?
Brother, he crops in the jungle still.
Where is the power that made your pride?
Brother, it ebbs from my flank and side.
Where is the haste that ye hurry by?
Brother, I go to my lair to die!

'Tiger! Tiger!'

Veil them, cover them, wall them round—
Blossom, and creeper, and weed—
Let us forget the sight and the sound,
The smell and the touch of the breed?

235

Fat black ash by the altar-stone,
    Here is the white-foot rain,
And the does bring forth in the fields unsown,
    And noon shall affright them again;
And the blind walls crumble, unknown, o'erthrown,
    And none shall inhabit again!

                  'Letting in the Jungle.'

These are the Four that are never content, that have
    never been filled since the Dews began—
Jacala's mouth, and the glut of the Kite, and the hands
    of the Ape, and the Eyes of Man.

                  'The King's Ankus.'

For our white and our excellent nights—for the nights of
    swift running,
Fair ranging, far-seeing, good hunting, sure cunning!
For the smells of the dawning, untainted, ere dew has
    departed!
For the rush through the mist, and the quarry blind-
    started!
For the cry of our mates when the sambhur has wheeled
    and is standing at bay!
        For the risk and the riot of night!
        For the sleep at the lair-mouth by day!
        It is met, and we go to the fight.
            Bay! O bay!

                  'Red Dog.'

Man goes to Man! Cry the challenge through the Jun-
    gle!
He that was our Brother goes away.
Hear, now, and judge, O ye People of the Jungle,—
Answer, who shall turn him—who shall stay?

CHAPTER HEADINGS

Man goes to Man! He is weeping in the Jungle:
  He that was our Brother sorrows sore!
Man goes to Man! (Oh, we loved him in the Jungle!)
  To the Man-Trail where we may not follow more.
'The Spring Running.'

At the hole where he went in
Red-Eye called to Wrinkle-Skin.
Hear what little Red-Eye saith:
'Nag, come up and dance with death!'

Eye to eye and head to head,
  (Keep the measure, Nag.)
This shall end when one is dead;
  (At thy pleasure, Nag.)

Turn for turn and twist for twist—
  (Run and hide thee, Nag.)
Hah! The hooded Death has missed!
  (Woe betide thee, Nag!)
'Rikki-Tikki-Tavi.'

Oh! hush thee, my baby, the night is behind us,
  And black are the waters that sparkled so green.
The moon, o'er the combers, looks downward to find us
  At rest in the hollows that rustle between.
Where billow meets billow, there soft be thy pillow;
  Ah, weary wee flipperling, curl at thy ease!
The storm shall not wake thee, nor shark overtake thee,
  Asleep in the arms of the slow-swinging seas.
'The White Seal.'

237

You mustn't swim till you're six weeks old,
　　Or your head will be sunk by your heels;
And summer gales and Killer Whales
　　Are bad for baby seals.
Are bad for baby seals, dear rat,
　　As bad as bad can be;
But splash and grow strong,
And you can't be wrong,
　　Child of the Open Sea!

　　　　　　　　　　'The White Seal.'

I will remember what I was, I am sick of rope and chain.
　　I will remember my old strength and all my forest
　　　　affairs.
I will not sell my back to man for a bundle of sugar-cane.
　　I will go out to my own kind, and the wood-folk in
　　　　their lairs.

I will go out until the day, until the morning break,
　　Out to the winds' untainted kiss, the waters' clean
　　　　caress.
I will forget my ankle-ring and snap my picket-stake.
　　I will revisit my lost loves, and playmates masterless!

　　　　　　　　　　'Toomai of the Elephants.'

The People of the Eastern Ice, they are melting like the
　　snow—
They beg for coffee and sugar; they go where the white
　　men go.
The People of the Western Ice, they learn to steal and
　　fight;
They sell their furs to the trading-post; they sell their
　　souls to the white.

The People of the Southern Ice, they trade with the
    whaler's crew;
Their women have many ribbons, but their tents are
    torn and few.
But the People of the Elder Ice, beyond the white man's
    ken—
Their spears are made of the narwhal-horn, and they are
    the last of the Men!

'Quiquern.'

When ye say to Tabaqui, 'My Brother!' when ye call
    the Hyena to meat,
Ye may cry the Full Truce with Jacala—the Belly that
    runs on four feet.

'The Undertakers.'

    The night we felt the earth would move
      We stole and plucked him by the hand,
    Because we loved him with the love
      That knows but cannot understand.

    And when the roaring hillside broke,
      And all our world fell down in rain,
    We saved him, we the Little Folk;
      But lo! he does not come again!

    Mourn now, we saved him for the sake
      Of such poor love as wild ones may.
    Mourn ye!   Our brother will not wake,
      And his own kind drive us away!

'The Miracle of Purun Bhagat.'

239

POSEIDON'S LAW

WHEN the robust and Brass-bound Man commissioned first for sea
His fragile raft, Poseidon laughed, and 'Mariner,' said he,
'Behold, a Law immutable I lay on thee and thine,
That never shall ye act or tell a falsehood at my shrine.

'Let Zeus adjudge your landward kin whose votive meal and salt
At easy-cheated altars win oblivion for the fault,
But you the unhoodwinked wave shall test—the immediate gulf condemn—
Except ye owe the Fates a jest, be slow to jest with them.

'Ye shall not clear by Greekly speech, nor cozen from your path
The twinkling shoal, the leeward beach, and Hadria's white-lipped wrath;
Nor tempt with painted cloth for wood my fraud-avenging hosts;
Nor make at all, or all make good, your bulwarks and your boasts.

'Now and henceforward serve unshod, through wet and wakeful shifts,
A present and oppressive God, but take, to aid, my gifts—

The wide and windward-opening eye, the large and lav-
ish hand,
The soul that cannot tell a lie—except upon the land!'

In dromond and in catafract—wet, wakeful, windward-
eyed—
He kept Poseidon's Law intact (his ship and freight
beside),
But, once discharged the dromond's hold, the bireme
beached once more,
Splendaciously mendacious rolled the Brass-bound Man
ashore.

The thranite now and thalamite are pressures low and
high,
And where three hundred blades bit white the twin-
propellers ply:
The God that hailed, the keel that sailed, are changed
beyond recall,
But the robust and Brass-bound Man he is not changed
at all!

From Punt returned, from Phormio's Fleet, from Javan
and Gadire,
He strongly occupies the seat about the tavern fire,
And, moist with much Falernian or smoked Massilian
juice,
Revenges there the Brass-bound Man his long-enforced
truce!

A TRUTHFUL SONG

THE Bricklayer:
    I tell this tale, which is strictly true,
    Just by way of convincing you
How very little, since things were made,
Things have altered in the building trade.

A year ago, come the middle of March,
We was building flats near the Marble Arch,
When a thin young man with coal-black hair
Came up to watch us working there.

Now there wasn't a trick in brick or stone
That this young man hadn't seen or known;
Nor there wasn't a tool from trowel to maul
But this young man could use 'em all!

Then up and spoke the plumbyers bold,
Which was laying the pipes for the hot and cold;
'Since you with us have made so free,
Will you kindly say what your name might be?'

The young man kindly answered them:
'It might be Lot or Methusalem,
Or it might be Moses (a man I hate),
Whereas it is Pharaoh surnamed the Great.

242

A TRUTHFUL SONG

'Your glazing is new and your plumbing's strange,
But otherwise I perceive no change,
And in less than a month if you do as I bid
I'd learn you to build me a Pyramid!'

The Sailor:
    I tell this tale, which is stricter true,
    Just by way of convincing you
    How very little, since things was made,
    Things have altered in the shipwright's trade.

In Blackwall Basin yesterday
A China barque re-fitting lay;
When a fat old man with snow-white hair
Came up to watch us working there.

Now there wasn't a knot which the riggers knew
But the old man made it—and better too;
Nor there wasn't a sheet, or a lift, or a brace,
But the old man knew its lead and place.

Then up and spake the caulkyers bold,
Which was packing the pump in the after-hold;
'Since you with us have made so free,
Will you kindly tell what your name might be?'

The old man kindly answered them:
'It might be Japheth, it might be Shem,
Or it might be Ham (though his skin was dark),
Whereas it is Noah, commanding the Ark.

'Your wheel is new and your pumps are strange,
But otherwise I perceive no change,
And in less than a week, if she did not ground,
I'd sail this hooker the wide world round!'

Both:
We tell these tales, which are strictest true,
Just by way of convincing you,
How very little, since things was made,
Anything alters in any one's trade.

SONGS FROM BOOKS

A SMUGGLERS' SONG

IF you wake at midnight, and hear a horse's feet,
  Don't go drawing back the blind, or looking in the
  street.
Them that ask no questions isn't told a lie.
Watch the wall, my darling, while the Gentlemen go by!
        Five and twenty ponies,
        Trotting through the dark—
        Brandy for the Parson,
        'Baccy for the Clerk;
        Laces for a lady, letters for a spy,
And watch the wall, my darling, while the Gentlemen
  go by!

Running round the woodlump if you chance to find
Little barrels, roped and tarred, all full of brandy-wine,
Don't you shout to come and look, nor use 'em for your
  play.
Put the brishwood back again—and they'll be gone next
  day!

If you see the stable-door setting open wide;
If you see a tired horse lying down inside;
If your mother mends a coat cut about and tore;
If the lining's wet and warm—don't you ask no more!

245

If you meet King George's men, dressed in blue and red,
You be careful what you say, and mindful what is said.
If they call you 'pretty maid,' and chuck you 'neath the
    chin,
Don't you tell where no one is, nor yet where no one's
    been!

Knocks and footsteps round the house—whistles after
    dark—
You've no call for running out till the house-dogs bark.
Trusty's here, and Pincher's here, and see how dumb
    they lie—
They don't fret to follow when the Gentlemen go by!

If you do as you've been told, 'likely there's a chance,
You'll be give a dainty doll, all the way from France,
With a cap of Valenciennes, and a velvet hood—
A present from the Gentlemen, along o' being good!
        Five and twenty ponies,
        Trotting through the dark,
        Brandy for the Parson,
        'Baccy for the Clerk.
Them that asks no questions isn't told a lie—
Watch the wall, my darling, while the Gentlemen go by!

(A. D. 1487)

HARRY, our King in England, from London town
    is gone,
    And comen to Hamull on the Hoke in the
    countie of Suthampton.
For there lay 'The Mary of the Tower,' his ship of war
    so strong,
And he would discover, certaynely, if his shipwrights did
    him wrong.

He told not none of his setting forth, nor yet where he
    would go,
(But only my Lord of Arundel), and meanly did he show,
In an old jerkin and patched hose that no man might
    him mark,
With his frieze hood and cloak above, he looked like any
    clerk.

He was at Hamull on the Hoke about the hour of the
    tide,
And saw the 'Mary' haled into dock, the winter to abide,
With all her tackle and habiliments which are the King
    his own;
But then ran on his false shipwrights and stripped her
    to the bone.

They heaved the main-mast overboard, that was of a
    trusty tree,
And they wrote down it was spent and lost by force of
    weather at sea.
But they sawen it into planks and strakes as far as it
    might go,
To maken beds for their own wives and little children also.

There was a knave called Slingawai, he crope beneath
    the deck,
Crying: 'Good felawes, come and see!   The ship is nigh
    a wreck!
For the storm that took our tall main-mast, it blew so
    fierce and fell,
Alack! it hath taken the kettles and pans, and this brass
    pott as well!'

With that he set the pott on his head and hied him up
    the hatch,
While all the shipwrights ran below to find what they
    might snatch;
All except Bob Brygandyne and he was a yeoman good,
He caught Slingawai round the waist and threw him on
    to the mud.

'I have taken plank and rope and nail, without the King
    his leave,
After the custom of Portesmouth, but I will not suffer a
    thief.
Nay, never lift up thy hand at me!   There's no clean
    hands in the trade—
Steal in measure,' quo' Brygandyne.   'There's measure
    in all things made!'

248

'Gramercy, yeoman!' said our King. 'Thy counsel
liketh me.'
And he pulled a whistle out of his neck and whistled
whistles three.
Then came my Lord of Arundel pricking across the
down,
And behind him the Mayor and Burgesses of merry
Suthampton town.

They drew the naughty shipwrights up, with the kettles
in their hands,
And bound them round the forecastle to wait the King's
commands.
But 'Since ye have made your beds,' said the King, 'ye
needs must lie thereon.
For the sake of your wives and little ones—felawes, get
you gone!'

When they had beaten Slingawai, out of his own lips,
Our King appointed Brygandyne to be Clerk of all his
ships.
'Nay, never lift up thy hands to me—there's no clean
hands in the trade.
But steal in measure,' said Harry our King. 'There's
measure in all things made!'

God speed the 'Mary of the Tower,' the 'Sovereign' and
'Grace Dieu,'
The 'Sweepstakes' and the 'Mary Fortune,' and the
'Henry of Bristol' too!
All tall ships that sail on the sea, or in our harbours
stand,
That they may keep measure with Harry our King and
peace in Engeland!

All ...

That they ...
pe...

THE SONG OF THE MACHINES

WE were taken from the ore-bed and the mine,
    We were melted in the furnace and the pit—
We were cast and wrought and hammered
    to design,
We were cut and filed and tooled and gauged to fit.
Some water, coal, and oil is all we ask,
    And a thousandth of an inch to give us play,
And now if you will set us to our task,
    We will serve you four-and-twenty hours a day!

    We can pull and haul and push and lift and drive,
        We can print and plough and weave and heat and
            light,
    We can run and jump and swim and fly and dive,
        We can see and hear and count and read and write!

Would you call a friend from half across the world?
    If you'll let us have his name and town and state,
You shall see and hear your crackling question hurled
    Across the arch of heaven while you wait.
Has he answered? Does he need you at his side?
    You can start this very evening if you choose,
And take the Western Ocean in the stride
    Of thirty thousand horses and some screws!

THE SONG OF THE MACHINES

The boat-express is waiting your command!
   You will find the 'Mauretania' at the quay,
Till her captain turns the lever 'neath his hand,
   And the monstrous nine-decked city goes to sea.

Do you wish to make the mountains bare their head
   And lay their new-cut forests at your feet?
Do you want to turn a river in its bed,
   And plant a barren wilderness with wheat?
Shall we pipe aloft and bring you water down
   From the never-failing cisterns of the Snows,
To work the mills and tramways in your town,
   And irrigate your orchards as it flows?

    It is easy! Give us dynamite and drills!
    Watch the iron-shouldered rocks lie down and
      quake
    As the thirsty desert-level floods and fills,
    And the valley we have dammed becomes a lake!

But remember, please, the Law by which we live,
   We are not built to comprehend a lie,
We can neither love nor pity nor forgive,
   If you make a slip in handling us you die!
We are greater than the Peoples or the Kings—
   Be humble, as you crawl beneath our rods!—
Our touch can alter all created things,
   We are everything on earth—except The Gods!

    Though our smoke may hide the Heavens from
      your eyes,
    It will vanish and the stars will shine again,
    Because, for all our power and weight and size,
    We are nothing more than children of your brain!

251

your eyes

It will vanish and the stars will shine again,

Because, for all

We are nothing more

THE WET LITANY

WHEN the water's countenance
Blurrs 'twixt glance and second glance;
When our tattered smokes forerun,
Ashen 'neath a silvered sun;
When the curtain of the haze
Shuts upon our helpless ways—
    Hear the Channel Fleet at sea;
    Libera nos Domine!

When the engines' bated pulse
Scarcely thrills the nosing hulls;
When the wash along the side
Sounds, a sudden, magnified;
When the intolerable blast
Marks each blindfold minute passed;

When the fog-buoy's squattering flight
Guides us through the haggard night;
When the warning bugle blows;
When the lettered doorways close;
When our brittle townships press,
Impotent, on emptiness;

When the unseen leadsmen lean
Questioning a deep unseen;

THE WET LITANY

When their lessened count they tell
To a bridge invisible;
When the hid and perilous
Cliffs return our cry to us;

When the treble thickness spread
Swallows up our next-ahead;
When her siren's frightened whine
Shows her sheering out of line;
When, her passage undiscerned,
We must turn where she has turned,
 Hear the Channel Fleet at sea;
 Libera nos Domine!

BIG STEAMERS

O H, where are you going to, all you Big Steamers,
    With England's own coal, up and down the
    salt seas?'
'We are going to fetch you your bread and your butter,
    Your beef, pork, and mutton, eggs, apples, and cheese.'

'And where will you fetch it from, all you Big Steamers,
    And where shall I write you when you are away?'
'We fetch it from Melbourne, Quebec, and Vancouver,
    Address us at Hobart, Hong-Kong, and Bombay.'

'But if anything happened to all you Big Steamers,
    And suppose you were wrecked up and down the salt
    sea?'
'Why you'd have no coffee or bacon for breakfast,
    And you'd have no muffins or toast for your tea.'

'Then I'll pray for fine weather for all you Big Steamers,
    For little blue billows and breezes so soft.'
'Oh, billows and breezes don't bother Big Steamers,
    For we're iron below and steel-rigging aloft.'

'Then I'll build a new lighthouse for all you Big Steamers,
    With plenty wise pilots to pilot you through.'
'Oh, the Channel's as bright as a ball-room already,
    And pilots are thicker than pilchards at Looe.'

BIG STEAMERS

'Then what can I do for you, all you Big Steamers,
  Oh, what can I do for your comfort and good?'
'Send out your big warships to watch your big waters,
  That no one may stop us from bringing you food.

'For the bread that you eat and the biscuits you nibble,
  The sweets that you suck and the joints that you
    carve,
They are brought to you daily by all us Big Steamers,
  And if any one hinders our coming you'll starve!'

THE BALLAD OF MINEPIT SHAW

ABOUT the time that taverns shut
    And men can buy no beer,
Two lads went up by the keepers' hut
    To steal Lord Pelham's deer.

Night and the liquor was in their heads—
    They laughed and talked no bounds,
Till they waked the keepers on their beds
    And the keepers loosed the hounds.

They had killed a hart, they had killed a hind,
    Ready to carry away,
When they heard a whimper down the wind
    And they heard a bloodhound bay.

They took and ran amongst the fern,
    Their crossbows in their hand,
Till they met a man with a green lantern
    That called and bade 'em stand.

'What are ye doing, O Flesh and Blood,
    And what's your foolish will,
That you must break into Minepit Wood
    And wake the Folk of the Hill?'

256

THE BALLAD OF MINEPIT SHAW

'Oh, we've broke into Lord Pelham's park,
   And killed Lord Pelham's deer,
And if ever you heard a little dog bark
   You'll know why we come here.

'We ask you let us go our way,
   As fast as we can flee,
For if ever you heard a bloodhound bay
   You'll know how pressed we be.'

'Oh, lay your crossbows on the bank
   And drop the knife from your hand,
And though the hounds are at your flank
   I'll save you where you stand!'

They laid their crossbows on the bank,
   They threw their knives in the wood,
And the ground before them opened and sank
   And saved 'em where they stood.

'Oh, what's the roaring in our ears
   That strikes us well-nigh dumb?'
'Oh, that is just how things appears
   According as they come.'

'What are the stars before our eyes
   That strike us well-nigh blind?'
'Oh, that is just how things arise
   According as you find.'

'And why's our bed so hard to the bones
   Excepting where it's cold?'
'Oh, that's because it is precious stones
   Excepting where 'tis gold.

'Think it over as you stand,
  For I tell you without fail,
If you haven't got into Fairyland
  You're not in Lewes Gaol.'

All night long they thought of it,
  And, come the dawn, they saw
They'd tumbled into a great old pit,
  At the bottom of Minepit Shaw.

And the keepers' hound had followed 'em close,
  And broke her neck in the fall;
So they picked up their knives and their crossbows
  And buried the dog.   That's all.

But whether the man was a poacher too
  Or a Pharisee[1] so bold—
I reckon there's more things told than are true,
  And more things true than are told!

[1]A fairy.

'Next day—next day! Unloose my cords!'

HERIOT'S FORD

'WHAT'S that that hirples at my side?'
 The foe that you must fight, my lord.
'That rides as fast as I can ride?'
 The shadow of your might, my lord.

'Then wheel my horse against the foe!'
 He's down and overpast, my lord.
You war against the sunset glow,
 The judgment follows fast, my lord.

'Oh who will stay the sun's descent?'
 King Joshua he is dead, my lord.
'I need an hour to repent!'
 'Tis what our sister said, my lord.

'Oh do not slay me in my sins!'
 You're safe awhile with us, my lord.
'Nay, kill me ere my fear begins!'
 We would not serve you thus, my lord.

'Where is the doom that I must face?'
 Three little leagues away, my lord.
'Then mend the horses' laggard pace!'
 We need them for next day, my lord.

'Next day—next day! Unloose my cords!'
  Our sister needed none, my lord.
You have no mind to face our swords,
  And—where can cowards run, my lord?

'You would not kill the soul alive?'
  'Twas thus our sister cried, my lord.
'I dare not die with none to shrive,'
  But so our sister died, my lord.

'Then wipe the sweat from brow and cheek,'
  It runnels forth afresh, my lord.
'Uphold me—for the flesh is weak.'
  You've finished with the Flesh, my lord.

FRANKIE'S TRADE

O LD Horn to All Atlantic said:
    (A-hay O! To me O!)
    'Now where did Frankie learn his trade?
For he ran me down with a three-reef mains'le.'
    (All round the Horn!)

Atlantic answered:—'Not from me!
You'd better ask the cold North Sea,
For he ran me down under all plain canvas.'
    (All round the Horn!)

The North Sea answered:—'He's my man,
For he came to me when he began—
Frankie Drake in an open coaster.'
    (All round the Sands!)

'I caught him young and I used him sore,
So you never shall startle Frankie more,
Without capsizing Earth and her waters.'
    (All round the Sands!)

'I did not favour him at all.
I made him pull and I made him haul—
And stand his trick with the common sailors.
    (All round the Sands!)

261

'I froze him stiff and I fogged him blind,
And kicked him home with his road to find
By what he could see in a three-day snow-storm.
   (All round the Sands!)

'I learned him his trade o' winter nights,
'Twixt Mardyk Fort and Dunkirk lights
On a five-knot tide with the forts a-firing.
   (All round the Sands!)

'Before his beard began to shoot,
I showed him the length of the Spaniard's foot—
And I reckon he clapped the boot on it later.
   (All round the Sands!)

'If there's a risk which you can make,
That's worse than he was used to take
Nigh every week in the way of his business;
    (All round the Sands!)

'If there's a trick that you can try,
Which he hasn't met in time gone by,
Not once or twice, but ten times over;
    (All round the Sands!)

'If you can teach him aught that's new,
    (A-hay O! To me O!)
I'll give you Bruges and Niewport too,
And the ten tall churches that stand between 'em,'
    Storm along, my gallant Captains!
    (All round the Horn!)

WITH DRAKE IN THE TROPICS

SOUTH and far south below the Line,
　　Our Admiral leads us on,
　Above, undreamed-of planets shine—
　　The stars we knew are gone.
Around, our clustered seamen mark
　The silent deep ablaze
With fires, through which the far-down shark
　Shoots glimmering on his ways.

The sultry tropic breezes fail
　That plagued us all day through;
Like molten silver hangs our sail,
　Our decks are dark with dew.
Now the rank moon commands the sky,
　Ho!　Bid the watch beware
And rouse all sleeping men that lie
　Unsheltered in her glare.

How long the time 'twixt bell and bell!
　How still our lanthorns burn!
How strange our whispered words that tell
　Of England and return!
Old towns, old streets, old friends, old loves,
　We name them each to each,
While the lit face of Heaven removes
　Them farther from our reach.

Now is the utmost ebb of night
  When mind and body sink,
And loneliness and gathering fright
  O'erwhelm us, if we think—
Yet, look, where in his room apart,
  All windows opened wide,
Our Admiral thrusts away the chart
  And comes to walk outside.

Kindly, from man to man he goes,
  With comfort, praise, or jest,
Quick to suspect our childish woes,
  Our terror and unrest.
It is as though the sun should shine—
  Our midnight fears are gone!
South and far south below the Line
  Our Admiral leads us on!

THE JUGGLER'S SONG

WHEN the drums begin to beat
      Down the street,
      When the poles are fetched and guyed,
When the tight-rope's stretched and tied,
When the dance-girls make salaam,
When the snake-bag wakes alarm,
When the pipes set up their drone,
When the sharp-edged knives are thrown,
When the red-hot coals are shown,
To be swallowed by and by—
Arre Brethren, here come I!

Stripped to loin-cloth in the sun
Search me well and watch me close!
Tell me how my tricks are done—
Tell me how the mango grows?

Give a man who is not made
      To his trade
Swords to fling and catch again,
Coins to ring and snatch again,
Men to harm and cure again,
Snakes to charm and lure again—
He'll be hurt by his own blade,
By his serpents disobeyed,
By his clumsiness bewrayed,

By the people laughed to scorn.
So 'tis not with juggler born!
Pinch of dust or withered flower,
Chance-flung nut or borrowed staff,
Serve his need and shore his power,
Bind the spell or loose the laugh!

THORKILD'S SONG

THERE'S no wind along these seas,
  Out oars for Stavanger!
  Forward all for Stavanger!
So we must wake the white-ash breeze,
  Let fall for Stavanger!
  A long pull for Stavanger!

Oh, hear the benches creak and strain!
  (A long pull for Stavanger!)
She thinks she smells the Northland rain!
  (A long pull for Stavanger!)

She thinks she smells the Northland snow,
And she's as glad as we to go.

She thinks she smells the Northland rime,
And the dear dark nights of winter-time.

She wants to be at her own home pier,
To shift her sails and standing gear.

She wants to be in her winter-shed,
To strip herself and go to bed.

Her very bolts are sick for shore,
And we—we want it ten times more!

267

So all you Gods that love brave men,
Send us a three-reef gale again!

Send us a gale, and watch us come,
With close-cropped canvas slashing home!

But—there's no wind on all these seas,
    A long pull for Stavanger!
So we must wake the white-ash breeze,
    A long pull for Stavanger!

SONGS FROM BOOKS

Au jana! Aua! Oha! Haq!
Back from the edge of the floe!

'ANGUTIVAUN TAINA'

Song of the Returning Hunter (Esquimaux)

OUR gloves are stiff with the frozen blood,
  Our furs with the drifted snow,
    As we come in with the seal—the seal!
  In from the edge of the floe.

Au jana! Aua! Oha! Haq!
  And the yelping dog-teams go,
And the long whips crack, and the men come back,
  Back from the edge of the floe!

We tracked our seal to his secret place,
  We heard him scratch below,
We made our mark, and we watched beside,
  Out on the edge of the floe.

We raised our lance when he rose to breathe,
  We drove it downward—so!
And we played him thus, and we killed him thus,
  Out on the edge of the floe.

Our gloves are glued with the frozen blood,
  Our eyes with the drifting snow;
But we come back to our wives again,
  Back from the edge of the floe!

Au jana! Aua! Oha! Haq!
And the loaded dog-teams go,
And the wives can hear their men come back,
Back from the edge of the floe!

SONG OF THE MEN'S SIDE

(Neolithic)

ONCE we feared The Beast—when he followed us
    we ran,
    Ran very fast though we knew
It was not right that The Beast should master Man;
    But what could we Flint-workers do?
The Beast only grinned at our spears round his ears—
    Grinned at the hammers that we made;
But now we will hunt him for the life with the Knife—
    And this is the Buyer of the Blade!

    Room for his shadow on the grass—let it pass!
        To left and right—stand clear!
    This is the Buyer of the Blade—be afraid!
        This is the great god Tyr!

Tyr thought hard till he hammered out a plan,
    For he knew it was not right
(And it is not right) that The Beast should master Man;
    So he went to the Children of the Night.
He begged a Magic Knife of their make for our sake.
    When he begged for the Knife they said:
'The price of the Knife you would buy is an eye!'
    And that was the price he paid.

Tell it to the Barrows of the Dead—run ahead!
  Shout it so the Women's Side can hear!
This is the Buyer of the Blade—be afraid!
  This is the great god Tyr!

Our women and our little ones may walk on the Chalk,
  As far as we can see them and beyond.
We shall not be anxious for our sheep when we keep
  Tally at the shearing-pond.
We can eat with both our elbows on our knees, if we
    please,
  We can sleep after meals in the sun;
For Shepherd of the Twilight is dismayed at the Blade,
  Feet-in-the-Night have run!
Dog-without-a-Master goes away (Hai, Tyr aie!),
  Devil-in-the-Dusk has run!

Then:
  Room for his shadow on the grass—let it pass!
    To left and right—stand clear!
  This is the Buyer of the Blade—be afraid!
    This is the great god Tyr!

    Rikki, with eyeballs of red!

DARZEE'S CHAUNT

(Sung in honour of Rikki-tikki-tavi)

SINGER and tailor am I—
    Doubled the joys that I know—
Proud of my lilt to the sky,
    Proud of the house that I sew—
Over and under, so weave I my music—so weave I the
    house that I sew.

Sing to your fledglings again,
    Mother, O lift up your head!
Evil that plagued us is slain,
    Death in the garden lies dead.
Terror that hid in the roses is impotent—flung on the
    dunghill and dead!

Who hath delivered us, who?
    Tell me his nest and his name.
Rikki, the valiant, the true,
    Tikki, with eyeballs of flame,
Rik-tikki-tikki, the ivory-fanged, the hunter with eye-
    balls of flame.

Give him the Thanks of the Birds,
    Bowing with tail-feathers spread!

273

Praise him with nightingale-words—
Nay, I will praise him instead.
Hear! I will sing you the praise of the bottle-tailed
Rikki, with eyeballs of red!

(Here Rikki-tikki interrupted, and the rest of the song
is lost.)

274

THE FOUR ANGELS

A S Adam lay a-dreaming beneath the Apple Tree
  The Angel of the Earth came down, and offered
  Earth in fee.
   But Adam did not need it,
   Nor the plough he would not speed it,
 Singing:—'Earth and Water, Air and Fire,
    What more can mortal man desire?'
    (The Apple Tree's in bud.)

As Adam lay a-dreaming beneath the Apple Tree
The Angel of the Waters offered all the Seas in fee.
   But Adam would not take 'em,
   Nor the ships he wouldn't make 'em,
 Singing:—'Water, Earth and Air and Fire,
    What more can mortal man desire?'
    (The Apple Tree's in leaf.)

As Adam lay a-dreaming beneath the Apple Tree
The Angel of the Air he offered all the Air in fee.
   But Adam did not crave it,
   Nor the flight he wouldn't brave it,
 Singing:—'Air and Water, Earth and Fire,
    What more can mortal man desire?'
    (The Apple Tree's in bloom.)

As Adam lay a-dreaming beneath the Apple Tree
The Angel of the Fire rose up and not a word said he.
    But he wished a flame and made it,
    And in Adam's heart he laid it,
  Singing:—'Fire, Fire, burning Fire,
        Stand up and reach your heart's desire!'
      (The Apple Blossom's set.)

As Adam was a-working outside of Eden-Wall,
He used the Earth, he used the Seas, he used the Air and
    all;
    And out of black disaster
    He arose to be the master
      Of Earth and Water, Air and Fire,
      But never reached his heart's desire!
      (The Apple Tree's cut down!)

THE GLORY OF THE GARDEN

OUR England is a garden that is full of stately views,
    Of borders, beds and shrubberies and lawns and
       avenues,
With statues on the terraces and peacocks strutting by;
But the Glory of the Garden lies in more than meets the
    eye.

For where the old thick laurels grow, along the thin red
    wall,
You'll find the tool- and potting-sheds which are the
    heart of all—
The cold-frames and the hot-houses, the dungpits and
    the tanks,
The rollers, carts and drain-pipes, with the barrows and
    the planks.

And there you'll see the gardeners, the men and 'pren-
    tice boys
Told off to do as they are bid and do it without noise;
For, except when seeds are planted and we shout to
    scare the birds,
The Glory of the Garden it abideth not in words.

And some can pot begonias and some can bud a rose,
And some are hardly fit to trust with anything that
    grows;

But they can roll and trim the lawns and sift the sand
    and loam,
For the Glory of the Garden occupieth all who come.

Our England is a garden, and such gardens are not made
By singing:—'Oh, how beautiful,' and sitting in the
    shade,
While better men than we go out and start their working
    lives
At grubbing weeds from gravel-paths with broken din-
    ner-knives.

There's not a pair of legs so thin, there's not a head so
    thick,
There's not a hand so weak and white, nor yet a heart
    so sick,
But it can find some needful job that's crying to be done,
For the Glory of the Garden glorifieth every one.

Then seek your job with thankfulness and work till
    further orders,
If it's only netting strawberries or killing slugs on bor-
    ders;
And when your back stops aching and your hands begin
    to harden,
You will find yourself a partner in the Glory of the
    Garden.

Oh, Adam was a gardener, and God Who made him sees
That half a proper gardener's work is done upon his knees,
So when your work is finished, you can wash your hands
    and pray
For the Glory of the Garden that it may not pass away!
And the Glory of the Garden it shall never pass away!

THE PRAYER

MY brother kneels, so saith Kabir,
    To stone and brass in heathen-wise,
    But in my brother's voice I hear
    My own unanswered agonies.
His God is as his fates assign,
His prayer is all the world's—and mine!

THE END

THE YEARS BETWEEN
AND PARODIES

TO THE SEVEN WATCHMEN

SEVEN watchmen sitting in a tower,
    Watching what had come upon mankind,
    Showed the Man the Glory and the Power,
And bade him shape the Kingdom to his mind.
'All things on Earth your will shall win you,'
    ('Twas so their counsel ran)
'But the Kingdom—the Kingdom is within you,'
    Said the Man's own mind to the Man.
                    For time, and some time—
As it was in the bitter years before
    So it shall be in the over-sweetened hour—
That a man's mind is wont to tell him more
    Than Seven Watchmen sitting in a tower.

CONTENTS

CONTENTS

CONTENTS

INDEX TO FIRST LINES

INDEX TO FIRST LINES

INDEX TO FIRST LINES

THE YEARS BETWEEN
AND PARODIES

THE ROWERS

1902

(When Germany proposed that England should help
her in a naval demonstration to collect debts from
Venezuela.)

THE banked oars fell an hundred strong,
  And backed and threshed and ground,
  But bitter was the rowers' song
As they brought the war-boat round.

They had no heart for the rally and roar
  That makes the whale-bath smoke—
When the great blades cleave and hold and leave
  As one on the racing stroke.

They sang:—'What reckoning do you keep,
  And steer by her what star,
If we come unscathed from the Southern deep
  To be wrecked on a Baltic bar?

'Last night you swore our voyage was done,
  But seaward still we go.
And you tell us now of a secret vow
  You have made with an open foe!

3

'That we must lie off a lightless coast
  And haul and back and veer,
At the will of the breed that have wronged us most
  For a year and a year and a year!

'There was never a shame in Christendie
  They laid not to our door—
And you say we must take the winter sea
  And sail with them once more?

'Look South! The gale is scarce o'erpast
  That stripped and laid us down,
When we stood forth but they stood fast
  And prayed to see us drown.

'Our dead they mocked are scarcely cold,
  Our wounds are bleeding yet—
And you tell us now that our strength is sold
  To help them press for a debt!

''Neath all the flags of all mankind
  That use upon the seas,
Was there no other fleet to find
  That you strike hands with these?

'Of evil times that men can choose
  On evil fate to fall,
What brooding Judgment let you loose
  To pick the worst of all?

THE ROWERS

'In sight of peace—from the Narrow Seas
  O'er half the world to run—
With a cheated crew, to league anew
  With the Goth and the shameless Hun!'

THE VETERANS

(Written for the gathering of survivors of the Indian Mutiny, Albert Hall, 1907.)

TO-DAY, across our fathers' graves,
    The astonished years reveal
    The remnant of that desperate host
Which cleansed our East with steel.

Hail and farewell! We greet you here,
    With tears that none will scorn—
O Keepers of the House of old,
    Or ever we were born!

One service more we dare to ask—
    Pray for us, heroes, pray,
That when Fate lays on us our task
    We do not shame the Day!

THE DECLARATION OF LONDON

JUNE 29, 1911

('On the re-assembling of Parliament after the Coronation, the Government have no intention of allowing their followers to vote according to their convictions on the Declaration of London, but insist on a strictly party vote.'—*Daily Papers*.)

WE were all one heart and one race
    When the Abbey trumpets blew.
    For a moment's breathing-space
We had forgotten you.
Now you return to your honoured place
    Panting to shame us anew.

We have walked with the Ages dead—
    With our Past alive and ablaze.
And you bid us pawn our honour for bread,
    This day of all the days!
And you cannot wait till our guests are sped,
    Or last week's wreath decays?

The light is still in our eyes
    Of Faith and Gentlehood,
Of Service and Sacrifice;
    And it does not match our mood,

7

To turn so soon to your treacheries
  That starve our land of her food.

Our ears still carry the sound
  Of our once Imperial seas,
Exultant after our King was crowned,
  Beneath the sun and the breeze.
It is too early to have them bound
  Or sold at your decrees.

Wait till the memory goes,
  Wait till the visions fade,
We may betray in time, God knows,
  But we would not have it said,
When you make report to our scornful foes,
  That we kissed as we betrayed!

8

ULSTER

1912

('Their webs shall not become garments, neither shall
they cover themselves with their works: their
works are works of iniquity and the act of violence
is in their hands.'—*Isaiah* lix. 6.)

THE dark eleventh hour
 Draws on and sees us sold
 To every evil power
We fought against of old.
Rebellion, rapine, hate,
Oppression, wrong and greed
Are loosed to rule our fate,
By England's act and deed.

The Faith in which we stand,
The laws we made and guard,
Our honour, lives, and land
Are given for reward
To Murder done by night,
To Treason taught by day,
To folly, sloth, and spite,
And we are thrust away.

9

The blood our fathers spilt,
Our love, our toils, our pains,
Are counted us for guilt,
And only bind our chains.
Before an Empire's eyes
The traitor claims his price.
What need of further lies?
We are the sacrifice.

We asked no more than leave
To reap where we had sown,
Through good and ill to cleave
To our own flag and throne.
Now England's shot and steel
Beneath that flag must show
How loyal hearts should kneel
To England's oldest foe.

We know the war prepared
On every peaceful home,
We know the hells declared
For such as serve not Rome—
The terror, threats, and dread
In market, hearth, and field—
We know, when all is said,
We perish if we yield.

Believe, we dare not boast,
Believe, we do not fear—
We stand to pay the cost
In all that men hold dear.

10

ULSTER

What answer from the North?
One Law, one Land, one Throne.
If England drive us forth
We shall not fall alone.

THE COVENANT

1914

WE thought we ranked above the chance of ill.
　　Others might fall, not we, for we were wise—
　　Merchants in freedom. So, of our free-will
We let our servants drug our strength with lies.
The pleasure and the poison had its way
　　On us as on the meanest, till we learned
That he who lies will steal, who steals will slay.
　　Neither God's judgment nor man's heart was turned.

Yet there remains His Mercy—to be sought
Through wrath and peril till we cleanse the wrong
By that last right which our forefathers claimed
When their Law failed them and its stewards were
　　bought.
This is our cause. God help us, and make strong
Our wills to meet Him later, unashamed!

FRANCE

1913

*B*ROKE *to every known mischance, lifted over all*
By the light sane joy of life, the buckler of the Gaul;
Furious in luxury, merciless in toil,
Terrible with strength that draws from her tireless soil;
Strictest judge of her own worth, gentlest of man's mind,
First to follow Truth and last to leave old Truths behind—
France, beloved of every soul that loves its fellow-kind!

Ere our birth (rememberest thou?) side by side we lay
Fretting in the womb of Rome to begin our fray.
Ere men knew our tongues apart, our one task was
known—
Each must mould the other's fate as he wrought his
own.
To this end we stirred mankind till all Earth was ours,
Till our world-end strifes begat wayside thrones and
powers—
Puppets that we made or broke to bar the other's path—
Necessary, outpost folk, hirelings of our wrath.
To this end we stormed the seas, tack for tack, and
burst
Through the doorways of new worlds, doubtful which
was first,
Hand on hilt (rememberest thou?) ready for the blow—

13

Sure, whatever else we met, we should meet our foe.
Spurred or baulked at every stride by the other's
    strength,
So we rode the ages down and every ocean's length!

Where did you refrain from us or we refrain from you?
Ask the wave that has not watched war between us two
Others held us for a while, but with weaker charms,
These we quitted at the call for each other's arms.
Eager toward the known delight, equally we strove—
Each the other's mystery, terror, need, and love.
To each other's open court with our proofs we came.
Where could we find honour else, or men to test our
    claim?
From each other's throat we wrenched—valour's last
    reward—
That extorted word of praise gasped 'twixt lunge and
    guard.
In each other's cup we poured mingled blood and tears,
Brutal joys, unmeasured hopes, intolerable fears—
All that soiled or salted life for a thousand years.
Proved beyond the need of proof, matched in every
    clime,
O companion, we have lived greatly through all time!

Yoked in knowledge and remorse, now we come to rest,
Laughing at old villainies that Time has turned to jest;
Pardoning old necessities no pardon can efface—
That undying sin we shared in Rouen market-place.
Now we watch the new years shape, wondering if they
    hold
Fiercer lightnings in their heart than we launched of
    old.

FRANCE

Now we hear new voices rise, question, boast or gird,
As we raged (rememberest thou?) when our crowds were
    stirred.
Now we count new keels afloat, and new hosts on land,
Massed like ours (rememberest thou?) when our strokes
    were planned.
We were schooled for dear life's sake, to know each
    other's blade.
What can blood and iron make more than we have
    made?
We have learned by keenest use to know each other's
    mind.
What shall blood and iron loose that we cannot bind?
We who swept each other's coast, sacked each other's
    home,
Since the sword of Brennus clashed on the scales at
    Rome
Listen, count and close again, wheeling girth to girth,
In the linked and steadfast guard set for peace on earth

Broke to every known mischance, lifted over all
By the light sane joy of life, the buckler of the Gaul;
Furious in luxury, merciless in toil,
Terrible with strength renewed from a tireless soil;
Strictest judge of her own worth, gentlest of man's
    mind,
First to face the Truth and last to leave old Truths
    behind—
France, beloved of every soul that loves or serves its
    kind!

'FOR ALL WE HAVE AND ARE'

1914

FOR all we have and are,
  For all our children's fate,
  Stand up and take the war,
The Hun is at the gate!
Our world has passed away,
In wantonness o'erthrown.
There is nothing left to-day
But steel and fire and stone!
    Though all we knew depart,
    The old Commandments stand:—
    'In courage keep your heart,
    In strength lift up your hand.'

Once more we hear the word
That sickened earth of old:—
'No law except the Sword
Unsheathed and uncontrolled.'
Once more it knits mankind,
Once more the nations go
To meet and break and bind
A crazed and driven foe.

16

'FOR ALL WE HAVE AND ARE'

Comfort, content, delight,
The ages' slow-bought gain,
They shrivelled in a night.
Only ourselves remain
To face the naked days
In silent fortitude,
Through perils and dismays
Renewed and re-renewed.
　　Though all we made depart,
　　The old Commandments stand:—
　　'In patience keep your heart,
　　In strength lift up your hand.'

No easy hope or lies
Shall bring us to our goal,
But iron sacrifice
Of body, will, and soul.
There is but one task for all—
One life for each to give.
Who stands if Freedom fall?
Who dies if England live?

A SONG IN STORM

BE well assured that on our side
    The abiding oceans fight,
    Though headlong wind and heaping tide
Make us their sport to-night.
By force of weather not of war
    In jeopardy we steer,
Then welcome Fate's discourtesy
    Whereby it shall appear,
      How in all time of our distress,
      And our deliverance too,
      The game is more than the player of the game,
      And the ship is more than the crew.

Out of the mist into the mirk
    The glimmering combers roll.
Almost these mindless waters work
    As though they had a soul—
Almost as though they leagued to whelm
    Our flag beneath their green:
Then welcome Fate's discourtesy
    Whereby it shall be seen, etc.

Be well assured, though wave and wind
    Have weightier blows in store,
That we who keep the watch assigned
    Must stand to it the more;

A SONG IN STORM

And as our streaming bows rebuke
    Each billow's baulked career,
Sing, welcome Fate's discourtesy
    Whereby it is made clear, etc.

No matter though our deck be swept
    And masts and timber crack—
We can make good all loss except
    The loss of turning back.
So, 'twixt these Devils and our deep
    Let courteous trumpets sound,
To welcome Fate's discourtesy
    Whereby it will be found, etc.

Be well assured, though in our power
    Is nothing left to give
But chance and place to meet the hour,
    And leave to strive to live,
Till these dissolve our Order holds,
    Our Service binds us here.
Then welcome Fate's discourtesy
    Whereby it is made clear,
        How in all time of our distress,
        And in our triumph too,
        The game is more than the player of the game,
        And the ship is more than the crew!

THE OUTLAWS

1914

T HROUGH learned and laborious years
    They set themselves to find
    Fresh terrors and undreamed-of fears
To heap upon mankind.

All that they drew from Heaven above
    Or digged from earth beneath,
They laid into their treasure-trove
    And arsenals of death:

While, for well-weighed advantage sake,
    Ruler and ruled alike
Built up the faith they meant to break
    When the fit hour should strike.

They traded with the careless earth,
    And good return it gave;
They plotted by their neighbour's hearth
    The means to make him slave.

When all was ready to their hand
  They loosed their hidden sword,
And utterly laid waste a land
  Their oath was pledged to guard.

Coldly they went about to raise
  To life and make more dread
Abominations of old days,
  That men believed were dead.

They paid the price to reach their goal
  Across a world in flame;
But their own hate slew their own soul
  Before that victory came.

ZION

THE Doorkeepers of Zion,
 They do not always stand
 In helmet and whole armour,
With halberds in their hand;
But, being sure of Zion,
 And all her mysteries,
They rest awhile in Zion,
Sit down and smile in Zion;
Ay, even jest in Zion;
 In Zion, at their ease.

The Gatekeepers of Baal,
 They dare not sit or lean,
But fume and fret and posture
 And foam and curse between;
For being bound to Baal,
 Whose sacrifice is vain,
Their rest is scant with Baal,
They glare and pant for Baal,
They mouth and rant for Baal,
 For Baal in their pain!

22

ZION

But we will go to Zion,
By choice and not through dread,
With these our present comrades
And those our present dead;
And, being free of Zion
In both her fellowships,
Sit down and sup in Zion—
Stand up and drink in Zion
Whatever cup in Zion
Is offered to our lips!

LORD ROBERTS

1914

HE passed in the very battle-smoke
  Of the war that he had descried.
Three hundred mile of cannon spoke
When the Master-Gunner died.

He passed to the very sound of the guns;
  But, before his eye grew dim,
He had seen the faces of the sons
  Whose sires had served with him.

He had touched their sword-hilts and greeted each
  With the old sure word of praise;
And there was virtue in touch and speech
  As it had been in old days.

So he dismissed them and took his rest,
  And the steadfast spirit went forth
Between the adoring East and West
  And the tireless guns of the North.

24

LORD ROBERTS

Clean, simple, valiant, well-beloved,
  Flawless in faith and fame,
Whom neither ease nor honours moved
  An hair's-breadth from his aim.

Never again the war-wise face,
  The weighed and urgent word
That pleaded in the market-place—
  Pleaded and was not heard!

Yet from his life a new life springs
  Through all the hosts to come,
And Glory is the least of things
  That follow this man home.

THE QUESTION

1916

BRETHREN, how shall it fare with me
　　When the war is laid aside,
　If it be proven that I am he
For whom a world has died?

If it be proven that all my good,
　And the greater good I will make,
Were purchased me by a multitude
　Who suffered for my sake?

That I was delivered by mere mankind
　Vowed to one sacrifice,
And not, as I hold them, battle-blind,
　But dying with open eyes?

That they did not ask me to draw the sword
　When they stood to endure their lot—
That they only looked to me for a word,
　And I answered I knew them not?

26

THE QUESTION

If it be found, when the battle clears,
    Their death has set me free,
Then how shall I live with myself through the years
    Which they have bought for me?

Brethren, how must it fare with me,
    Or how am I justified,
If it be proven that I am he
    For whom mankind has died;
If it be proven that I am he
    Who being questioned denied?

THE CHOICE

1917

(THE AMERICAN SPIRIT SPEAKS)

*T*O *the Judge of Right and Wrong*
 With Whom fulfilment lies
 Our purpose and our power belong,
Our faith and sacrifice.

Let Freedom's Land rejoice!
 Our ancient bonds are riven;
Once more to us the eternal choice
 Of Good or Ill is given.

Not at a little cost,
 Hardly by prayer or tears,
Shall we recover the road we lost
 In the drugged and doubting years.

But, after the fires and the wrath,
 But, after searching and pain,
His Mercy opens us a path
 To live with ourselves again.

28

THE CHOICE

In the Gates of Death rejoice!
    We see and hold the good—
Bear witness, Earth, we have made our choice
    With Freedom's brotherhood!

Then praise the Lord Most High
    Whose Strength hath saved us whole,
Who bade us choose that the Flesh should die
    And not the living Soul!

To the God in Man displayed—
    Where e'er we see that Birth,
Be love and understanding paid
    As never yet on earth !

To the Spirit that moves in Man,
    On Whom all worlds depend,
Be Glory since our world began
    And service to the end !

THE HOLY WAR

1917

('For here lay the excellent wisdom of him that built
Mansoul, that the walls could never be broken
down nor hurt by the most mighty adverse poten-
tate unless the townsmen gave consent thereto.'—
BUNYAN'S *Holy War*.)

A TINKER out of Bedford,
    A vagrant oft in quod,
    A private under Fairfax,
A minister of God—
Two hundred years and thirty
    Ere Armageddon came
His single hand portrayed it,
    And Bunyan was his name !

He mapped, for those who follow,
    The world in which we are—
'This famous town of Mansoul'
    That takes the Holy War.

Her true and traitor people,
    The gates along her wall,
From Eye Gate unto Feel Gate,
    John Bunyan showed them all.

All enemy divisions.
  Recruits of every class,
And highly-screened positions
  For flame or poison-gas;
The craft that we call modern,
  The crimes that we call new,
John Bunyan had 'em typed and filed
  In Sixteen, Eighty-two.

Likewise the Lords of Looseness
  That hamper faith and works,
The Perseverance-Doubters,
  And Present-Comfort shirks,
With brittle intellectuals
  Who crack beneath a strain—
John Bunyan met that helpful set
  In Charles the Second's reign.

Emmanuel's vanguard dying
  For right and not for rights,
My Lord Apollyon lying
  To the State-kept Stockholmites,
The Pope, the swithering Neutrals,
  The Kaiser and his Gott—
Their rôles, their goals, their naked souls—
  He knew and drew the lot.

Now he hath left his quarters,
  In Bunhill Fields to lie,
The wisdom that he taught us
  Is proven prophecy—

One watchword through our armies,
  One answer from our lands:—
'No dealings with Diabolus
  As long as Mansoul stands!'

A pedlar from a hovel,
  The lowest of the low,
The father of the Novel,
  Salvation's first Defoe,
Eight blinded generations
  Ere Armageddon came,
He showed us how to meet it,
  And Bunyan was his name!

THE HOUSES

(A SONG OF THE DOMINIONS)

1898

TWIXT my house and thy house the pathway is
 broad,
 In thy house or my house is half the world's
hoard;
By my house and thy house hangs all the world's fate,
On thy house and my house lies half the world's hate.

For my house and thy house no help shall we find
Save thy house and my house—kin cleaving to kind;
If my house be taken, thine tumbleth anon,
If thy house be forfeit, mine followeth soon.

'Twixt my house and thy house what talk can there be
Of headship or lordship, or service or fee?
Since my house to thy house no greater can send
Than thy house to my house—friend comforting friend;
And thy house to my house no meaner can bring
Than my house to thy house—King counselling King.

RUSSIA TO THE PACIFISTS

GOD rest you, peaceful gentlemen, let nothing you
    dismay,
    But—leave your sports a little while—the dead
are borne this way!
Armies dead and Cities dead, past all count or care.
God rest you, merry gentlemen, what portent see you
    there?
      Singing:—Break ground for a wearied host
        That have no ground to keep.
        Give them the rest that they covet
        most . . .
        And who shall next to sleep, good sirs,
        In such a trench to sleep?

God rest you, peaceful gentlemen, but give us leave to
    pass.
We go to dig a nation's grave as great as England was.
For this Kingdom and this Glory and this Power and
    this Pride
Three hundred years it flourished—in three hundred
    days it died.

RUSSIA TO THE PACIFISTS

Singing:—Pour oil for a frozen throng,
That lie about the ways.
Give them the warmth they have
lacked so long . . .
And what shall be next to blaze, good
sirs,
On such a pyre to blaze?

God rest you, thoughtful gentlemen, and send your
sleep is light!
Remains of this dominion no shadow, sound, or sight,
Except the sound of weeping and the sight of burning
fire,
And the shadow of a people that is trampled into mire.
Singing:—Break bread for a starving folk
That perish in the field.
Give them their food as they take the
yoke . . .
And who shall be next to yield, good
sirs,
For such a bribe to yield?

God rest you, merry gentlemen, and keep you in your
mirth!
Was ever kingdom turned so soon to ashes, blood, and
earth?
'Twixt the summer and the snow—seeding-time and
frost—
Arms and victual, hope and counsel, name and country
lost!

Singing:—*Let down by the foot and the head—*
Shovel and smooth it all !
So do we bury a Nation dead . . .
And who shall be next to fall, good
sirs,
With your good help to fall?

THE IRISH GUARDS

1918

WE'RE not so old in the Army List,
   But we're not so young at our trade,
  For we had the honour at Fontenoy
Of meeting the Guards' Brigade.
'Twas Lally, Dillon, Bulkeley, Clare,
  And Lee that led us then,
And after a hundred and seventy years
  We're fighting for France again!
    Old Days!   The wild geese are flighting,
     Head to the storm as they faced it before!
    For where there are Irish there's bound to be fighting,
     And when there's no fighting, it's Ireland no more!
        Ireland no more!

The fashion's all for khaki now,
  But once through France we went
Full-dressed in scarlet Army cloth,
  The English—left at Ghent.
They're fighting on our side to-day
  But, before they changed their clothes,
The half of Europe knew our fame,
  As all of Ireland knows!

37

THE YEARS BETWEEN AND PARODIES

Old Days!   The wild geese are flying,
  Head to the storm as they faced it before!
For where there are Irish there's memory undying,
  And when we forget, it is Ireland no more!
                    Ireland no more!

From Barry Wood to Gouzeaucourt,
  From Boyne to Pilkem Ridge,
The ancient days come back no more
  Than water under the bridge.
But the bridge it stands and the water runs
  As red as yesterday,
And the Irish move to the sound of the guns
  Like salmon to the sea.
    Old Days!   The wild geese are ranging,
      Head to the storm as they faced it before!
    For where there are Irish their hearts are unchanging,
      And when they are changed, it is Ireland no more!
                    Ireland no more!

We're not so old in the Army List,
  But we're not so new in the ring,
For we carried our packs with Marshal Saxe
  When Louis was our King.
But Douglas Haig's our Marshal now
  And we're King George's men,
And after one hundred and seventy years
  We're fighting for France again!

38

Ah, France!   And did we stand by you,
  When life was made splendid with gifts and
    rewards?
Ah, France!   And will we deny you
  In the hour of your agony, Mother of Swords?
Old Days!   The wild geese are flighting,
  Head to the storm as they faced it before!
For where there are Irish there's loving and fighting,
  And when we stop either, it's Ireland no more!
                    Ireland no more!

A NATIVITY

1916

*T*HE *Babe was laid in the Manger*
  Between the gentle kine—
  All safe from cold and danger—
'But it was not so with mine.
                    (With mine!   With mine!)

'Is it well with the child, is it well?'
  The waiting mother prayed.
'For I know not how he fell,
  And I know not where he is laid.'

A Star stood forth in Heaven;
  The watchers ran to see
The Sign of the Promise given—
  'But there comes no sign to me.
                    (To me!   To me!)

'*My* child died in the dark.
  Is it well with the child, is it well?
There was none to tend him or mark,
  And I know not how he fell.'

A NATIVITY

The Cross was raised on high;
  The Mother grieved beside—
'But the Mother saw Him die
  And took Him when He died.
                    (He died! He died!)

'Seemly and undefiled
  His burial-place was made—
Is it well, is it well with the child?
  For I know not where he is laid.'

On the dawning of Easter Day
  Comes Mary Magdalene;
But the Stone was rolled away,
  And the Body was not within—
                    (Within! Within!)

'Ah, who will answer my word?'
  The broken mother prayed.
'They have taken away my Lord,
  And I know not where He is laid.'

   .   .   .   .   .

'The Star stands forth in Heaven.
  The watchers watch in vain
For a Sign of the Promise given
  Of peace on Earth again—
                    (Again! Again!)

'But I know for Whom he fell'—
  The steadfast mother smiled,
'Is it well with the child—is it well?
  It is well—it is well with the child!'

41

EN–DOR

('Behold there is a woman that hath a familiar spirit at
En-dor.'—1 *Samuel* xxviii. 7.)

THE road to En-dor is easy to tread
    For Mother or yearning Wife,
    There, it is sure, we shall meet our Dead
As they were even in life.
Earth has not dreamed of the blessing in store
For desolate hearts on the road to En-dor.

Whispers shall comfort us out of the dark—
    Hands—ah God!—that we knew!
Visions and voices—look and heark!—
    Shall prove that our tale is true,
And that those who have passed to the further shore
May be hailed—at a price—on the road to En-dor.

But they are so deep in their new eclipse
    Nothing they say can reach,
Unless it be uttered by alien lips
    And framed in a stranger's speech.
The son must send word to the mother that bore,
Through an hireling's mouth. 'Tis the rule of En-dor.

EN-DOR

And not for nothing these gifts are shown
　　By such as delight our dead.
They must twitch and stiffen and slaver and groan
　　Ere the eyes are set in the head,
And the voice from the belly begins.　Therefore,
We pay them a wage where they ply at En-dor.

Even so, we have need of faith
　　And patience to follow the clue.
Often, at first, what the dear one saith
　　Is babble, or jest, or untrue.
(Lying spirits perplex us sore
Till our loves—and our lives—are well-known at
　　En-dor). . . .

Oh the road to En-dor is the oldest road
　　And the craziest road of all !
Straight it runs to the Witch's abode,
　　As it did in the days of Saul,
And nothing has changed of the sorrow in store
For such as go down on the road to En-dor !

A RECANTATION

(TO LYDE OF THE MUSIC HALLS)

WHAT boots it on the Gods to call?
 Since, answered or unheard,
 We perish with the Gods and all
Things made—except the Word.

Ere certain Fate had touched a heart
 By fifty years made cold,
I judged thee, Lyde, and thy art
 O'erblown and over-bold.

But he—but he, of whom bereft
 I suffer vacant days—
He on his shield not meanly left—
 He cherished all thy lays.

Witness the magic coffer stocked
 With convoluted runes
Wherein thy very voice was locked
 And linked to circling tunes.

44

A RECANTATION

Witness thy portrait, smoke-defiled,
   That decked his shelter-place.
Life seemed more present, wrote the child,
   Beneath thy well-known face.

And when the grudging days restored
   Him for a breath to home,
He, with fresh crowds of youth, adored
   Thee making mirth in Rome.

Therefore, I, humble, join the hosts,
   Loyal and loud, who bow
To thee as Queen of Songs—and ghosts—
   For I remember how

Never more rampant rose the Hall
   At thy audacious line
Than when the news came in from Gaul
   Thy son had—followed mine.

But thou didst hide it in thy breast
   And, capering, took the brunt
Of blaze and blare, and launched the jest
   That swept next week the front.

Singer to children! Ours possessed
   Sleep before noon—but thee,
Wakeful each midnight for the rest,
   No holocaust shall free.

Yet they who use the Word assigned,
　To hearten and make whole,
Not less than Gods have served mankind,
　Though vultures rend their soul.

MY BOY JACK

'HAVE you news of my boy Jack?'
        Not this tide.
        'When d'you think that he'll come back?'
Not with this wind blowing, and this tide.

'Has any one else had word of him?'
    Not this tide.
For what is sunk will hardly swim,
    Not with this wind blowing, and this tide.

'Oh, dear, what comfort can I find?'
        None this tide,
        Nor any tide,
Except he did not shame his kind—
    Not even with that wind blowing, and that tide.

Then hold your head up all the more,
        This tide,
        And every tide;
Because he was the son you bore,
    And gave to that wind blowing and that tide!

47

THE VERDICTS

(JUTLAND)

NOT in the thick of the fight,
 Not in the press of the odds,
 Do the heroes come to their height,
Or we know the demi-gods.

That stands over till peace.
 We can only perceive
Men returned from the seas,
 Very grateful for leave.

They grant us sudden days
 Snatched from their business of war;
But we are too close to appraise
 What manner of men they are.

And, whether their names go down
 With age-kept victories,
Or whether they battle and drown
 Unreckoned, is hid from our eyes.

48

THE VERDICTS

They are too near to be great,
  But our children shall understand
When and how our fate
  Was changed, and by whose hand.

Our children shall measure their worth.
  We are content to be blind . . .
But we know that we walk on a new-born earth
  With the saviours of mankind.

MESOPOTAMIA

1917

THEY shall not return to us, the resolute, the
young,
  The eager and whole-hearted whom we gave:
But the men who left them thriftily to die in their own
dung,
  Shall they come with years and honour to the grave?

They shall not return to us, the strong men coldly slain
  In sight of help denied from day to day:
But the men who edged their agonies and chid them in
their pain,
  Are they too strong and wise to put away?

Our dead shall not return to us while Day and Night
divide—
  Never while the bars of sunset hold:
But the idle-minded overlings who quibbled while they
died,
  Shall they thrust for high employments as of old?

MESOPOTAMIA

Shall we only threaten and be angry for an hour?
  When the storm is ended shall we find
How softly but how swiftly they have sidled back to
    power
  By the favour and contrivance of their kind?

Even while they soothe us, while they promise large
    amends,
  Even while they make a show of fear,
Do they call upon their debtors, and take council with
    their friends,
  To confirm and re-establish each career?

Their lives cannot repay us—their death could not
    undo—
  The shame that they have laid upon our race:
But the slothfulness that wasted and the arrogance that
    slew,
  Shall we leave it unabated in its place?

THE HYÆNAS

AFTER the burial-parties leave
　　And the baffled kites have fled;
　　The wise hyænas come out at eve
To take account of our dead.

How he died and why he died
　　Troubles them not a whit.
They snout the bushes and stones aside
　　And dig till they come to it.

They are only resolute they shall eat
　　That they and their mates may thrive,
And they know that the dead are safer meat
　　Than the weakest thing alive.

(For a goat may butt, and a worm may sting,
　　And a child will sometimes stand;
But a poor dead soldier of the King
　　Can never lift a hand.)

They whoop and halloo and scatter the dirt
　　Until their tushes white
Take good hold in the army shirt,
　　And tug the corpse to light.

And the pitiful face is shewn again
   For an instant ere they close;
But it is not discovered to living men—
   Only to God and to those

Who, being soulless, are free from shame,
   Whatever meat they may find.
Nor do they defile the dead man's name—
   That is reserved for his kind.

THE SPIES' MARCH

(BEFORE THE WAR)

('The outbreak is in full swing and our death-rate
would sicken Napoleon. . . . Dr. M—— died
last week, and C—— on Monday, but some more
medicines are coming. . . . We don't seem to
be able to check it at all. . . . Villages panick-
ing badly. . . . In some places not a living
soul. . . . But at any rate the experience
gained may come in useful, so I am keeping my
notes written up to date in case of accidents.
. . . Death is a queer chap to live with for
steady company.'—*Extract from a private letter
from Manchuria.*)

THERE are no leaders to lead us to honour, and
yet without leaders we sally,
Each man reporting for duty alone, out of sight,
out of reach, of his fellow.
There are no bugles to call the battalions, and yet
without bugles we rally
From the ends of the earth to the ends of the earth,
to follow the Standard of Yellow!
Fall in! O fall in! O fall in!

Not where the squadrons mass,
Not where the bayonets shine,

54

THE SPIES' MARCH

Not where the big shell shout as they pass
    Over the firing-line;
Not where the wounded are,
    Not where the nations die,
Killed in the cleanly game of war—
    That is no place for a spy!
O Princes, Thrones and Powers, your work is less
    than ours—
Here is no place for a spy!

Trained to another use,
    We march with colours furled,
Only concerned when Death breaks loose
    On a front of half a world.
Only for General Death
    The Yellow Flag may fly,
While we take post beneath—
    That is the place for a spy.
Where Plague has spread his pinions over Nations
    and Dominions—
Then will be work for a spy!

The dropping shots begin,
    The single funerals pass,
Our skirmishers run in,
    The corpses dot the grass!
The howling towns stampede,
    The tainted hamlets die.
Now it is war indeed—
    Now there is room for a spy!

O Peoples, Kings and Lands, we are waiting you
    commands—
What is the work for a spy?
    (DRUMS)—*Fear is upon us, spy!*

'Go where his pickets hide—
    Unmask the shapes they take,
Whether a gnat from the waterside,
    Or stinging fly in the brake,
Or filth of the crowded street,
    Or a sick rat limping by,
Or a smear of spittle dried in the heat—
    That is the work of a spy!
        (DRUMS)—*Death is upon us, spy!*

'What does he next prepare?
    Whence will he move to attack?—
By water, earth or air?—
    How can we head him back?
Shall we starve him out if we burn
    Or bury his food-supply?
Slip through his lines and learn—
    That is work for a spy!
        (DRUMS)—*Get to your business, spy!*

'Does he feint or strike in force?
    Will he charge or ambuscade?
What is it checks his course?
    Is he beaten or only delayed?

THE SPIES' MARCH

How long will the lull endure?
  Is he retreating?   Why?
Crawl to his camp and make sure—
  That is the work for a spy!
      (Drums)—*Fetch us our answer, spy!*

'Ride with him girth to girth
  Wherever the Pale Horse wheels,
Wait on his councils, ear to earth,
  And say what the dust reveals.
For the smoke of our torment rolls
  Where the burning thousands lie;
What do we care for men's bodies or souls?
  Bring us deliverance, spy!'

THE SONS OF MARTHA

THE Sons of Mary seldom bother, for they hav
inherited that good part;
But the Sons of Martha favour their Mother o
the careful soul and the troubled heart.
And because she lost her temper once, and because sh
was rude to the Lord her Guest,
Her Sons must wait upon Mary's Sons, world withou
end, reprieve, or rest.

It is their care in all the ages to take the buffet and
cushion the shock.
It is their care that the gear engages; it is their car
that the switches lock.
It is their care that the wheels run truly; it is their car
to embark and entrain,
Tally, transport, and deliver duly the Sons of Mary by
land and main.

They say to mountains, 'Be ye removèd.' They say
to the lesser floods 'Be dry.'
Under their rods are the rocks reprovèd—they are not
afraid of that which is high.

THE SONS OF MARTHA

Then do the hill-tops shake to the summit—then is the
bed of the deep laid bare,
That the Sons of Mary may overcome it, pleasantly
sleeping and unaware.

They finger death at their gloves' end where they
piece and repiece the living wires.
He rears against the gates they tend: they feed him
hungry behind their fires.
Early at dawn, ere men see clear, they stumble into
his terrible stall,
And hale him forth like a haltered steer, and goad and
turn him till evenfall.

To these from birth is Belief forbidden; from these till
death is Relief afar.
They are concerned with matters hidden—under the
earth-line their altars are:
The secret fountains to follow up, waters withdrawn
to restore to the mouth,
And gather the floods as in a cup, and pour them again
at a city's drouth.

They do not preach that their God will rouse them a
little before the nuts work loose.
They do not teach that His Pity allows them to leave
their work when they damn-well choose.
As in the thronged and the lighted ways, so in the
dark and the desert they stand,
Wary and watchful all their days that their brethren's
days may be long in the land.

Raise ye the stone or cleave the wood to make a pat
    more fair or flat;
Lo, it is black already with blood some Son of Marth
    spilled for that!
Not as a ladder from earth to Heaven, not as a witnes
    to any creed,
But simple service simply given to his own kind i
    their common need.

And the Sons of Mary smile and are blessèd—the
    know the angels are on their side.
They know in them is the Grace confessèd, and fo
    them are the Mercies multiplied.
They sit at the Feet—they hear the Word—they s
    how truly the Promise runs;
They have cast their burden upon the Lord, and—th
    Lord He lays it on Martha's Sons!

MARY'S SON

IF YOU stop to find out what your wages will be
   And how they will clothe and feed you,
  Willie, my son, don't you go on the Sea,
 For the Sea will never need you.

If you ask for the reason of every command,
   And argue with people about you,
Willie, my son, don't you go on the Land,
  For the Land will do better without you.

If you stop to consider the work you have done
   And to boast what your labour is worth, dear,
Angels may come for you, Willie, my son,
  But you'll never be wanted on Earth, dear!

THE SONG OF THE LATHES

1918

(Being the words of the tune hummed at her lathe b
Mrs. L. Embsay, widow.)

THE fans and the beltings they roar round me.
The power is shaking the floor round me
Till the lathes pick up their duty and the mic
night shift takes over.
It is good for me to be here!

Guns in Flanders—Flanders guns !
(I had a man that worked 'em once !)
Shells for guns in Flanders, Flanders !
Shells for guns in Flanders, Flanders !
>   *Shells for guns in Flanders !   Feed the guns !*

The cranes and the carriers they boom over me,
The bays and the galleries they loom over me,
With their quarter-mile of pillars growing little in th
distance:
It is good for me to be here!

THE SONG OF THE LATHES

The Zeppelins and Gothas they raid over us.
Our lights give warning, and fade over us.
(Seven thousand women keeping quiet in the darkness!)
       Oh, it is good for me to be here!

The roofs and the buildings they grow round me,
Eating up the fields I used to know round me;
And the shed that I began in is a sub-inspector's office—
       So long have I been here!

I've seen six hundred mornings make our lamps grow
    dim,
Through the bit that isn't painted round our skylight
    rim,
And the sunshine in the window slope according to the
    seasons,
       Twice since I've been here.

The trains on the sidings they call to us
With the hundred thousand blanks that they haul to us;
And we send 'em what we've finished, and they take
    it where it's wanted,
       For that is why we are here!

Man's hate passes as his love will pass.
God made woman what she always was.
Them that bear the burden they will never grant for-
    giveness
       So long as they are here!

63

THE YEARS BETWEEN AND PARODIES

Once I was a woman, but that's by with me.
All I loved and looked for, it must die with me.
But the Lord has left me over for a servant of the
      Judgment,
          And I serve His Judgments here!

Guns in Flanders—Flanders guns !
(I had a son that worked 'em once !)
Shells for guns in Flanders, Flanders !
Shells for guns in Flanders, Flanders !
      Shells for guns in Flanders !   Feed the guns !

GETHSEMANE

THE Garden called Gethsemane
   In Picardy it was,
And there the people came to see
The English soldiers pass.
We used to pass—we used to pass
   Or halt, as it might be,
And ship our masks in case of gas
   Beyond Gethsemane.

The Garden called Gethsemane,
   It held a pretty lass,
But all the time she talked to me
   I prayed my cup might pass.
The officer sat on the chair,
   The men lay on the grass,
And all the time we halted there
   I prayed my cup might pass.

It didn't pass—it didn't pass—
   It didn't pass from me.
I drank it when we met the gas
   Beyond Gethsemane.

THE PRO-CONSULS

THE overfaithful sword returns the user
  His heart's desire at price of his heart's blood.
The clamour of the arrogant accuser
Wastes that one hour we needed to make good.
This was foretold of old at our outgoing;
This we accepted who have squandered, knowing,
The strength and glory of our reputations,
At the day's need, as it were dross, to guard
The tender and new-dedicate foundations
Against the sea we fear—not man's award.

They that dig foundations deep,
    Fit for realms to rise upon,
Little honour do they reap
    Of their generation,
Any more than mountains gain
Stature till we reach the plain.

With no veil before their face
    Such as shroud or sceptre lend—
Daily in the market-place,
    Of one height to foe and friend—
They must cheapen self to find
Ends uncheapened for mankind.

THE PRO–CONSULS

Through the night when hirelings rest,
  Sleepless they arise, alone,
The unsleeping arch to test
  And the o'er-trusted corner-stone,
'Gainst the need, they know, that lies
Hid behind the centuries.

Not by lust of praise or show
  Not by Peace herself betrayed—
Peace herself must they forego
  Till that peace be fitly made;
And in single strength uphold
Wearier hands and hearts acold.

On the stage their act hath framed
  For thy sports, O Liberty!
Doubted are they, and defamed
  By the tongues their act set free,
While they quicken, tend and raise
Power that must their power displace.

Lesser men feign greater goals,
  Failing whereof they may sit
Scholarly to judge the souls
  That go down into the pit,
And, despite its certain clay,
Heave a new world towards the day.

These at labour make no sign,
  More than planets, tides or years
Which discover God's design,
  Not our hopes and not our fears;
Nor in aught they gain or lose
Seek a triumph or excuse.

For, so the Ark be borne to Zion, who
Heeds how they perished or were paid that bore it ?
For, so the Shrine abide, what shame—what pride—
If we, the priests, were bound or crowned before it ?

THE CRAFTSMAN

ONCE, after long-drawn revel at The Mermaid,
　　He to the overbearing Boanerges
　　Jonson, uttered (If half of it were liquor,
　　　　　Blessed be the vintage!)

Saying how, at an alehouse under Cotswold,
He had made sure of his very Cleopatra,
Drunk with enormous, salvation-contemning
　　　　　Love for a tinker.

How, while he hid from Sir Thomas's keepers,
Crouched in a ditch and drenched by the midnight
Dews, he had listened to gipsy Juliet
　　　　　Rail at the dawning.

How at Bankside, a boy drowning kittens
Winced at the business; whereupon his sister
(Lady Macbeth aged seven) thrust 'em under,
　　　　　Sombrely scornful.

How on a Sabbath, hushed and compassionate—
She being known since her birth to the townsfolk—
Stratford dredged and delivered from Avon
　　　　　Dripping Ophelia.

o, with a thin third finger marrying
Drop to wine-drop domed on the table,
Shakespeare opened his heart till sunrise
     Entered to hear him.

London wakened and he, imperturbable,
Passed from waking to hurry after shadows . . .
Busied upon shows of no earthly importance?
     Yes, but he knew it!

THINGS AND THE MAN

(IN MEMORIAM, JOSEPH CHAMBERLAIN)

1904

'And Joseph dreamed a dream, and he told it his
brethren: and they hated him yet the more.'—
Genesis xxxvii. 5.)

OH ye who hold the written clue
  To all save all unwritten things,
  And, half a league behind, pursue
The accomplished Fact with flouts and flings,
Look! To your knee your baby brings
  The oldest tale since Earth began—
  The answer to your worryings:
   'Once on a time there was a Man.'

He, single-handed, met and slew
  Magicians, Armies, Ogres, Kings.
He lonely 'mid his doubting crew—
  'In all the loneliness of wings'—
  He fed the flame, he filled the springs,
  He locked the ranks, he launched the van
Straight at the grinning Teeth of Things.
   'Once on a time there was a Man.'

The peace of shocked Foundations flew
 Before his ribald questionings.
He broke the Oracles in two,
 And bared the paltry wires and strings.
He headed desert wanderings;
  He led his soul, his cause, his clan
A little from the ruck of Things.
  'Once on a time there was a Man.'

Thrones, Powers, Dominions block the view
 With episodes and underlings—
The meek historian deems them true
 Nor heeds the song that Clio sings—
The simple central truth that stings
  The mob to boo, the priest to ban;
Things never yet created things—
  'Once on a time there was a Man.'

A bolt is fallen from the blue.
 A wakened realm full circle swings
Where Dothan's dreamer dreams anew
 Of vast and farborne harvestings;
And unto him an Empire clings
  That grips the purpose of his plan.
My Lords, how think you of these things?
  Once—in our time—is there a Man?

THE BENEFACTORS

*A*H ! *What avails the classic bent*
    And what the cultured word,
    Against the undoctored incident
That actually occurred ?

And what is Art whereto we press
    Through paint and prose and rhyme—
When Nature in her nakedness
    Defeats us every time ?

It is not learning, grace nor gear,
    Nor easy meat and drink,
But bitter pinch of pain and fear
    That makes creation think.

When in this world's unpleasing youth
    Our god-like race began,
The longest arm, the sharpest tooth,
    Gave man control of man;

73

Till, bruised and bitten to the bone
And taught by pain and fear,
He learned to deal the far-off stone,
And poke the long, safe spear.

So tooth and nail were obsolete
As means against a foe,
Till, bored by uniform defeat,
Some genius built the bow.

Then stone and javelin proved as vain
As old-time tooth and nail;
Ere, spurred anew by fear and pain,
Man fashioned coats of mail.

Then was there safety for the rich
And danger for the poor,
Till someone mixed a powder which
Redressed the scale once more.

Helmet and armour disappeared
With sword and bow and pike,
And, when the smoke of battle cleared,
All men were armed alike. . . .

And when ten million such were slain
To please one crazy king,
Man, schooled in bulk by fear and pain,
Grew weary of the thing;

THE BENEFACTORS

And, at the very hour designed,
  To enslave him past recall,
His tooth-stone-arrow-gun-shy mind
  Turned and abolished all.

.   .   .   .

All Power, each Tyrant, every Mob
  Whose head has grown too large,
Ends by destroying its own job
  And earns its own discharge.

And Man, whose mere necessities
  Move all things from his path,
Trembles meanwhile at their decrees,
  And deprecates their wrath !

THE DEAD KING

(EDWARD VII.)

1910

*W*HO *in the Realm to-day lays down dear life for
    the sake of a land more dear ?
    And, unconcerned for his own estate, toils till
    the last grudged sands have run ?
    Let him approach. It is proven here
Our King asks nothing of any man more than Our
King himself has done.*

For to him above all was Life good, above all he com-
    manded
        Her abundance full-handed.
The peculiar treasure of Kings was his for the taking:
All that men come to in dreams he inherited waking:—
His marvel of world-gathered armies—one heart and
    all races;
His seas 'neath his keels when his war-castles foamed
    to their places;
The thundering foreshores that answered his heralded
    landing;
The huge lighted cities adoring, the assemblies up-
    standing;

76

THE DEAD KING

The Councils of Kings called in haste to learn how he
    was minded—
The Kingdoms, the Powers, and the Glories he dealt
    with unblinded.

To him came all captains of men, all achievers of glory,
Hot from the press of their battles they told him their
    story.
They revealed him their life in an hour and, saluting,
    departed,
Joyful to labour afresh—he had made them new-
    hearted.
And, since he weighed men from his youth, and no lie
    long deceived him,
He spoke and exacted the truth, and the basest believed
    him.

And God poured him an exquisite wine, that was daily
    renewed to him,
In the clear-welling love of his peoples that daily ac-
    crued to him.
Honour and service we gave him, rejoicingly fearless;
Faith absolute, trust beyond speech and a friendship
    as peerless.
And since he was Master and Servant in all that we
    asked him,
We leaned hard on his wisdom in all things, knowing
    not how we tasked him.

For on him each new day laid command, every tyran-
    nous hour,
To confront, or confirm, or make smooth some dread
    issue of power;

To deliver true judgment aright at the instant, unaided,
In the strict, level, ultimate phrase that allowed or
dissuaded;
To foresee, to allay, to avert from us perils unnumbered,
To stand guard on our gates when he guessed that the
watchmen had slumbered;
To win time, to turn hate, to woo folly to service and,
mightily schooling
His strength to the use of his Nations, to rule as not
ruling.

These were the works of our King; Earth's peace was
the proof of them.
God gave him great works to fulfil, and to us the behoof
of them.
We accepted his toil as our right—none spared, none
excused him.
When he was bowed by his burden his rest was refused
him.
We troubled his age with our weakness—the blacker
our shame to us!
Hearing his People had need of him, straightway he
came to us.

As he received so he gave—nothing grudged, naught
denying,
Not even the last gasp of his breath when he strove for
us, dying.
For our sakes, without question, he put from him all
that he cherished.
Simply as any that serve him he served and he perished.
All that Kings covet was his, and he flung it aside for us.
Simply as any that die in his service he died for us.

THE DEAD KING

Who in the Realm to-day has choice of the easy road or
    the hard to tread ?
  And, much concerned for his own estate, would sell
    his soul to remain in the sun ?
      Let him depart nor look on Our dead.
  Our King asks nothing of any man more than Our
    King himself has done.

A DEATH-BED

'THIS is the State above the Law.
    The State exists for the State alone.'
    [*This is a gland at the back of the jaw,*
    And an answering lump by the collar-bone.]

Some die shouting in gas or fire;
    Some die silent, by shell and shot.
Some die desperate, caught on the wire;
    Some die suddenly.   This will not.

'Regis suprema Voluntas lex'
    [*It will follow the regular course of—throats.*]
Some die pinned by the broken decks,
    Some die sobbing between the boats.

Some die eloquent, pressed to death
    By the sliding trench as their friends can hear.
Some die wholly in half a breath.
    Some—give trouble for half a year.

'There is neither Evil nor Good in life
    Except as the needs of the State ordain.'
[*Since it is rather too late for the knife,*
    All we can do is to mask the pain.]

80

A DEATH-BED

Some die saintly in faith and hope—
　　One died thus in a prison-yard—
Some die broken by rape or the rope;
　　Some die easily.　　This dies hard.

'I will dash to pieces who bar my way.
　　Woe to the traitor!　　Woe to the weak!'
[*Let him write what he wishes to say.*
　　It tires him out if he tries to speak.]

Some die quietly.　　Some abound
　　In loud self-pity.　　Others spread
Bad morale through the cots around　.　.　.
　　This is a type that is better dead.

'The war was forced on me by my foes.
　　All that I sought was the right to live.'
[*Don't be afraid of a triple dose;*
　　The pain will neutralize half we give.

Here are the needles.　　See that he dies
　　While the effects of the drug endure.　.　.　.
What is the question he asks with his eyes?—
　　Yes, All-Highest, to God, be sure.]

81

GEHAZI

‘WHENCE comest thou, Gehazi
  So reverend to behold,
  In scarlet and in ermines
And chain of England's gold?’
‘From following after Naaman
  To tell him all is well,
Whereby, my zeal hath made me
A Judge in Israel.’

Well done, well done, Gehazi,
  Stretch forth thy ready hand,
Thou barely 'scaped from judgment,
  Take oath to judge the land,
Unswayed by gift of money
  Or privy bribe, more base,
Of knowledge which is profit
  In any market-place.

Search out and probe, Gehazi,
  As thou of all canst try,
The truthful, well-weighed answer
  That tells the blacker lie—

GEHAZI

The loud, uneasy virtue
  The anger feigned at will,
To overbear a witness
  And make the Court keep still.

Take order now, Gehazi,
  That no man talk aside
In secret with his judges
  The while his case is tried.
Lest he should show them—reason
  To keep a matter hid,
And subtly lead the questions
  Away from what he did.
Thou mirror of uprightness,
  What ails thee at thy vows?
What means the risen whiteness
  Of the skin between thy brows?

The boils that shine and burrow,
  The sores that slough and bleed—
The leprosy of Naaman
  On thee and all thy seed?
    Stand up, stand up, Gehazi,
      Draw close thy robe and go,
    Gehazi, Judge in Israel,
      A leper white as snow!

THE VIRGINITY

T RY as he will, no man breaks wholly loose
From his first love, no matter who she be.
Oh, was there ever sailor free to choose,
That didn't settle somewhere near the sea?

Myself, it don't excite me nor amuse
To watch a pack o' shipping on the sea,
But I can understand my neighbour's views
From certain things which have occurred to me.

Men must keep touch with things they used to use
To earn their living, even when they are free;
And so come back upon the least excuse—
Same as the sailor settled near the sea.

He knows he's never going on no cruise—
He knows he's done and finished with the sea;
And yet he likes to feel she's there to use—
If he should ask her—as she used to be.

THE VIRGINITY

Even though she cost him all he had to lose,
Even though she made him sick to hear or see,
Still, what she left of him will mostly choose
Her skirts to sit by.   How comes such to be?

Parsons in pulpits, tax-payers in pews,
Kings on your thrones, you know as well as me,
We've only one virginity to lose,
And where we lost it there our hearts will be !

A PILGRIM'S WAY

I DO not look for holy saints to guide me on my way,
   Or male and female devilkins to lead my feet
      astray.
If these are added, I rejoice—if not, I shall not mind,
So long as I have leave and choice to meet my fellow-
      kind.
   For as we come and as we go (and deadly soon go
      we!)
   The people, Lord, Thy people, are good enough for me!

Thus I will honour pious men whose virtue shines so
      bright
(Though none are more amazed than I when I by
      chance do right),
And I will pity foolish men for woe their sins have bred
(Though ninety-nine per cent. of mine I brought on
      my own head).
   And, Amorite or Eremite, or General Averagee,
   The people, Lord, Thy people, are good enough for
      me!

And when they bore me overmuch, I will not shake
      mine ears,
Recalling many thousand such whom I have bored to
      tears.

And when they labour to impress, I will not doubt
    nor scoff;
Since I myself have done no less and—sometimes
    pulled it off.
  Yea, as we are and we are not, and we pretend to be,
  The people, Lord, Thy people, are good enough for
    me!

And when they work me random wrong, as oftentimes
    hath been,
I will not cherish hate too long (my hands are none
    too clean).
And when they do me random good I will not feign
    surprise.
No more than those whom I have cheered with way-
    side charities.
  But, as we give and as we take—whate'er our tak-
    ings be—
  The people, Lord, Thy people, are good enough for
    me!

But when I meet with frantic folk who sinfully declare
There is no pardon for their sin, the same I will not
    spare
Till I have proved that Heaven and Hell which in our
    hearts we have
Show nothing irredeemable on either side the grave.
  For as we live and as we die—if utter Death there
    be—
  The people, Lord, Thy people, are good enough for
    me!

Deliver me from every pride—the Middle, High, and
Low—
That bars me from a brother's side, whatever state
he show.
And purge me from all heresies of thought and speech
and pen
That bid me judge him otherwise than I am judged.
Amen!

That I may sing of Crowd or King or road-borne
company,
That I may labour in my day, vocation and degree,
To prove the same in deed and name, and hold
unshakenly
(Where'er I go, whate'er I know, whoe'er my neigh-
bour be)
This single faith in Life and Death and all Eternity:
'The people, Lord, Thy people, are good enough
for me!'

THE OLDEST SONG

(For before Eve was Lilith.—*Old Tale.*)

THESE were never your true love's eyes.
  Why do you feign that you love them?
  You that broke from their constancies,
And the wide calm brows above them!

This was never your true love's speech.
  Why do you thrill when you hear it?
You that have ridden out of its reach
  The width of the world or near it!

This was never your true love's hair,—
  You that chafed when it bound you
Screened from knowledge or shame or care,
  In the night that it made around you!

'*All these things I know, I know.*
  And that's why my heart is breaking!'
Then what do you gain by pretending so?
  '*The joy of an old wound waking.*'

NATURAL THEOLOGY

PRIMITIVE

I ATE my fill of a whale that died
    And stranded after a month at sea. . . .
There is a pain in my inside.
    Why have the Gods afflicted me?
Ow!   I am purged till I am a wraith!
    Wow!   I am sick till I cannot see!
What is the sense of Religion and Faith?
    Look how the Gods have afflicted me!

PAGAN

How can the skin of rat or mouse hold
    Anything more than a harmless flea? . . .
The burning plague has taken my household.
    Why have my Gods afflicted me?
All my kith and kin are deceased,
    Though they were as good as good could be.
I will out and batter the family priest,
    Because my Gods have afflicted me.

90

NATURAL THEOLOGY

MEDIÆVAL

My privy and well drain into each other
   After the custom of Christendie. . . .
Fevers and fluxes are wasting my mother.
   Why has the Lord afflicted me?
The Saints are helpless for all I offer—
   So are the clergy I used to fee.
Henceforward I keep my cash in my coffer,
   Because the Lord has afflicted me.

MATERIAL

I run eight hundred hens to the acre.
   They die by dozens mysteriously. . . .
I am more than doubtful concerning my Maker.
   Why has the Lord afflicted me?
What a return for all my endeavour—
   Not to mention the L. S. D.!
I am an atheist now and for ever,
   Because this God has afflicted me!

PROGRESSIVE

Money spent on an Army or Fleet
   Is homicidal lunacy. . . .
My son has been killed in the Mons retreat.
   Why is the Lord afflicting me?
Why are murder, pillage and arson
   And rape allowed by the Deity?
I will write to the *Times*, deriding our parson,
   Because my God has afflicted me.

CHORUS

We had a kettle: we let it leak:
  Our not repairing it made it worse.
We haven't had any tea for a week. . . .
  The bottom is out of the Universe!

CONCLUSION

This was none of the good Lord's pleasure,
  For the Spirit He breathed in Man is free;
But what comes after is measure for measure,
  And not a God that afflicteth thee.
As was the sowing so the reaping
  Is now and evermore shall be.
Thou art delivered to thy own keeping.
  Only Thyself hath afflicted thee!

When the cock crew—when the cock crew,

The next time that Peter denied his Lord
As he sat by the fire and warmed himself through.
Then the cock crew! etc.

A SONG AT COCK–CROW

'Ille autem iterum negavit.'

THE first time that Peter deniéd his Lord
He shrank from the cudgel, the scourge and the
cord,
But followed far off to see what they would do,
Till the cock crew—till the cock crew—
After Gethsemane, till the cock crew!

The first time that Peter deniéd his Lord
'Twas only a maid in the palace who heard,
As he sat by the fire and warmed himself through.
Then the cock crew!   Then the cock crew!
('Thou also art one of them.')   Then the cock crew!

The first time that Peter deniéd his Lord
He had neither the Throne, nor the Keys nor the
Sword—
A poor silly fisherman, what could he do
When the cock crew—when the cock crew—
But weep for his wickedness when the cock crew?

. . . .

The next time that Peter deniéd his Lord
He was Fisher of Men, as foretold by the Word,

93

With the Crown on his brow and the Cross on his shoe,
When the cock crew—when the cock crew—
In Flanders and Picardy when the cock crew.

The next time that Peter deniéd his Lord
'Twas Mary the Mother in Heaven Who heard,
And She grieved for the maidens and wives that they
slew
When the cock crew—when the cock crew—
At Tirmonde and Aerschott when the cock crew.

The next time that Peter deniéd his Lord
The Babe in the Manger awakened and stirred,
And He stretched out His arms for the playmates He
knew—
When the cock crew—when the cock crew—
But the waters had covered them when the cock crew.

The next time that Peter deniéd his Lord
'Twas Earth in her agony waited his word,
But he sat by the fire and naught would he do,
Though the cock crew—though the cock crew—
Over all Christendom, though the cock crew.

The last time that Peter deniéd his Lord,
The Father took from him the Keys and the Sword,
And the Mother and Babe brake his Kingdom in two,
When the cock crew—when the cock crew—
(Because of his wickedness) when the cock crew !

THE FEMALE OF THE SPECIES

1911

WHEN the Himalayan peasant meets the he-
bear in his pride,
He shouts to scare the monster, who will often
turn aside.
But the she-bear thus accosted rends the peasant tooth
and nail.
For the female of the species is more deadly than the
male.

When Nag the basking cobra hears the careless foot
of man,
He will sometimes wriggle sideways and avoid it as he
can.
But his mate makes no such motion where she camps
beside the trail.
For the female of the species is more deadly than the
male.

When the early Jesuit fathers preached to Hurons and
Choctaws,
They prayed to be delivered from the vengeance of
the squaws.

'Twas the women, not the warriors, turned those stark
enthusiasts pale.
For the female of the species is more deadly than the
male.

Man's timid heart is bursting with the things he must
not say,
For the Woman that God gave him isn't his to give
away;
But when hunter meets with husband, each confirms the
other's tale—
The female of the species is more deadly than the male.

Man, a bear in most relations—worm and savage
otherwise,—
Man propounds negotiations, Man accepts the com-
promise.
Very rarely will he squarely push the logic of a fact
To its ultimate conclusion in unmitigated act.

Fear, or foolishness, impels him, ere he lay the wicked
low,
To concede some form of trial even to his fiercest foe.
Mirth obscene diverts his anger! Doubt and Pity
oft perplex
Him in dealing with an issue—to the scandal of The
Sex!

But the Woman that God gave him, every fibre of
her frame
Proves her launched for one sole issue, armed and
engined for the same;

THE FEMALE OF THE SPECIES

And to serve that single issue, lest the generations fail,
The female of the species must be deadlier than the
male.

She who faces Death by torture for each life beneath
her breast
May not deal in doubt or pity—must not swerve for
fact or jest.
These be purely male diversions—not in these her
honour dwells.
She the Other Law we live by, is that Law and nothing
else.

She can bring no more to living than the powers that
make her great
As the Mother of the Infant and the Mistress of the
Mate!
And when Babe and Man are lacking and she strides
unclaimed to claim
Her right as femme (and baron), her equipment is the
same.

She is wedded to convictions—in default of grosser ties;
Her contentions are her children, Heaven help him who
denies!—
He will meet no suave discussion, but the instant,
white-hot, wild,
Wakened female of the species warring as for spouse
and child.

Unprovoked and awful charges—even so the she-bear
fights,
Speech that drips, corrodes, and poisons—even so the
cobra bites,
Scientific vivisection of one nerve till it is raw
And the victim writhes in anguish—like the Jesuit with
the squaw!

So it comes that Man the coward, when he gathers to
confer
With his fellow-braves in council, dare not leave a
place for her
Where, at war with Life and Conscience, he uplifts
his erring hands
To some God of Abstract Justice—which no woman
understands.

And Man knows it! Knows, moreover, that the
Woman that God gave him
Must command but may not govern—shall enthral
but not enslave him.
And *She* knows, because She warns him, and Her
instincts never fail,
That the Female of Her Species is more deadly than
the Male.

EPITAPHS

'Equality of Sacrifice'

A. 'I was a "have."' *B.* 'I was a "have-not."'
(*Together*). 'What hast thou given which I gave not?'

A Servant

We were together since the War began.
He was my servant—and the better man.

A Son

My son was killed while laughing at some jest. I
  would I knew
What it was, and it might serve me in a time when
  jests are few.

An Only Son

I have slain none except my Mother. She
(Blessing her slayer) died of grief for me.

Ex-Clerk

Pity not! The Army gave
Freedom to a timid slave:
In which Freedom did he find
Strength of body, will, and mind:

By which strength he came to prove
Mirth, Companionship, and Love:
For which Love to Death he went:
In which Death he lies content.

THE WONDER

Body and Spirit I surrendered whole
To harsh Instructors—and received a soul . . .
If mortal man could change me through and through
From all I was—what may The God not do?

HINDU SEPOY IN FRANCE

This man in his own country prayed we know not to
    what Powers.
We pray Them to reward him for his bravery in ours.

THE COWARD

I could not look on Death, which being known,
Men led me to him, blindfold and alone.

SHOCK

My name, my speech, my self I had forgot.
My wife and children came—I knew them not.
I died.   My Mother followed.   At her call
And on her bosom I remembered all.

A GRAVE NEAR CAIRO

Gods of the Nile, should this stout fellow here
Get out—get out!   He knows not shame nor fear.

100

Pelicans in the Wilderness

(a grave near halfa)

The blown sand heaps on me, that none may learn
  Where I am laid for whom my children grieve. . .
O wings that beat at dawning, ye return
  Out of the desert to your young at eve!

The Favour

Death favoured me from the first, well knowing I
  could not endure
    To wait on him day by day.   He quitted my betters
    and came
Whistling over the fields, and, when he had made all
  sure,
    'Thy line is at end,' he said, 'but at least I have
    saved its name.'

The Beginner

On the first hour of my first day
  In the front trench I fell.
(Children in boxes at a play
  Stand up to watch it well.)

R. A. F. (Aged Eighteen)

Laughing through clouds, his milk-teeth still unshed,
Cities and men he smote from overhead.
His deaths delivered, he returned to play
Childlike, with childish things now put away.

THE REFINED MAN

I was of delicate mind. I went aside for my needs,
  Disdaining the common office. I was seen from afar
  and killed. . . .
How is this matter for mirth? Let each man be judged
  by his deeds.
*I have paid my price to live with myself on the terms
  that I willed.*

NATIVE WATER-CARRIER (M. E. F.)

Prometheus brought down fire to men.
  This brought up water.
The Gods are jealous—now, as then,
  They gave no quarter.

BOMBED IN LONDON

On land and sea I strove with anxious care
To escape conscription. It was in the air!

THE SLEEPY SENTINEL

Faithless the watch that I kept: now I have none to
  keep.
I was slain because I slept: now I am slain I sleep.
Let no man reproach me again, whatever watch is
  unkept—
I sleep because I am slain. They slew me because I
  slept.

EPITAPHS

Batteries out of Ammunition

If any mourn us in the workshop, say
We died because the shift kept holiday.

Common Form

If any question why we died,
Tell them, because our fathers lied.

A Dead Statesman

I could not dig: I dared not rob:
Therefore I lied to please the mob.
Now all my lies are proved untrue,
And I must face the men I slew.
What tale shall save me here among
Mine angry and defrauded young?

The Rebel

If I had clamoured at Thy Gate
  For gift of Life on Earth,
And, thrusting through the souls that wait,
  Flung headlong into birth—
Even then, even then, for gin and snare
  About my pathway spread,
Lord, I had mocked Thy thoughtful care
  Before I joined the Dead!
But now? . . . I was beneath Thy Hand
  Ere yet the Planets came.
And now—though Planets pass, I stand
  The witness to Thy shame.

THE YEARS BETWEEN AND PARODIES

THE OBEDIENT

Daily, though no ears attended,
 Did my prayers arise.
Daily, though no fire descended
 Did I sacrifice. . . .
Though my darkness did not lift,
 Though I faced no lighter odds,
Though the Gods bestowed no gift,
   None the less,
 None the less, I served the Gods!

A DRIFTER OFF TARENTUM

He from the wind-bitten north with ship and companions descended.
 Searching for eggs of death spawned by invisible hulls.
Many he found and drew forth. Of a sudden the fishery ended
 In flame and a clamorous breath not new to the eye-pecking gulls.

DESTROYERS IN COLLISION

For Fog and Fate no charm is found
 To lighten or amend.
I, hurrying to my bride, was drowned—
 Cut down by my best friend.

CONVOY ESCORT

I was a shepherd to fools
 Causelessly bold or afraid.

104

They would not abide by my rules.
Yet they escaped. For I stayed.

UNKNOWN FEMALE CORPSE

Headless, lacking foot and hand,
Horrible I come to land.
I beseech all women's sons
Know I was a mother once.

RAPED AND REVENGED

One used and butchered me: another spied
Me broken—for which thing a hundred died.
So it was learned among the heathen hosts
How much a freeborn woman's favour costs.

SALONIKAN GRAVE

I have watched a thousand days
Push out and crawl into night
Slowly as tortoises.
Now I, too, follow these.
It is fever, and not fight—
Time, not battle—that slays.

THE BRIDEGROOM

Call me not false, beloved,
  If, from thy scarce-known breast
So little time removed,
  In other arms I rest.

For this more ancient bride
　Whom coldly I embrace
Was constant at my side
　Before I saw thy face.

Our marriage, often set—
　By miracle delayed—
At last is consummate,
　And cannot be unmade.

Live, then, whom Life shall cure,
　Almost, of Memory,
And leave us to endure
　Its immortality.

V. A. D. (MEDITERRANEAN)

Ah, would swift ships had never been, for then w
　n'er had found,
These harsh Ægean rocks between, this little virgi
　drowned,
Whom neither spouse nor child shall mourn, but me
　she nursed through pain
And—certain keels for whose return the heathen loo.
　in vain.

'THE CITY OF BRASS'

1909

('Here was a people whom after their works thou shalt
see wept over for their lost dominion: and in this
palace is the last information respecting lords collected in the dust.'—*The Arabian Nights.*)

*IN a land that the sand overlays—the ways to her gates
are untrod—*
  *A multitude ended their days whose fates were made
splendid by God,*
*Till they grew drunk and were smitten with madness
and went to their fall,*
*And of these is a story written: but Allah alone knoweth
all !*

When the wine stirred in their heart their bosoms
    dilated,
They rose to suppose themselves kings over all things
    created—
To decree a new earth at a birth without labour or
    sorrow—
To declare: 'We prepare it to-day and inherit to-
    morrow.'

They chose themselves prophets and priests of minut
    understanding,
Men swift to see done, and outrun, their extremes
    commanding—
Of the tribe which describe with a jibe the perversion
    of Justice—
Panders avowed to the crowd whatsoever its lust is.

Swiftly these pulled down the walls that their father
    had made them—
The impregnable ramparts of old, they razed and relaid
    them
As playgrounds of pleasure and leisure with limitless
    entries,
And havens of rest for the wastrels where once walked
    the sentries;

And because there was need of more pay for the shouters
    and marchers,
They disbanded in face of their foemen their bowmen
    and archers.
They replied to their well-wishers' fears—to their
    enemies' laughter,
Saying: 'Peace! We have fashioned a God Which
    shall save us hereafter.
We ascribe all dominion to man in his factions con-
    ferring,
And have given to numbers the Name of the Wisdom
    unerring.'
They said: 'Who has hate in his soul? Who has
    envied his neighbour?
Let him arise and control both that man and his
    labour.'

They said: 'Who is eaten by sloth? Whose unthrift
    has destroyed him?
He shall levy a tribute from all because none have
    employed him.'
They said: 'Who hath toiled? Who hath striven,
    and gathered possession?
Let him be spoiled. He hath given full proof of trans-
    gression.'
They said: 'Who is irked by the Law? *Though
    we may not remove it,
If he lend us his aid in this raid, we will set him above
    it !*'
So the robber did judgment again upon such as dis-
    pleased him,
The slayer, too, boasted his slain, and the judges re-
    leased him,

As for their kinsmen far off, on the skirts of the nation,
They harried all earth to make sure none escaped
    reprobation,
They awakened unrest for a jest in their newly-won
    borders,
And jeered at the blood of their brethren betrayed by
    their orders.
They instructed the ruled to rebel, their rulers to aid
    them;
And, since such as obeyed them not fell, their Viceroys
    obeyed them.
When the riotous set them at naught they said: 'Praise
    the upheaval!
For the show and the word and the thought of Dominion
    is evil!'

They unwound and flung from them with rage, as :
rag that defiled them

The imperial gains of the age which their forefather
piled them.

They ran panting in haste to lay waste and embitte
for ever

The wellsprings of Wisdom and Strength which ar
Faith and Endeavour.

They nosed out and digged up and dragged forth and
exposed to derision

All doctrine of purpose and worth and restraint and
prevision:

And it ceased, and God granted them all things fo:
which they had striven,

And the heart of a beast in the place of a man's hear
was given. . . .

. . . .

When they were fullest of wine and most flagrant in
error,

Out of the sea rose a sign—out of Heaven a terror.

Then they saw, then they heard, then they knew—
for none troubled to hide it,

An host had prepared their destruction, but still they
denied it.

They denied what they dared not abide if it came to
the trial,

But the Sword that was forged while they lied did not
heed their denial.

It drove home, and no time was allowed to the crowd
that was driven.

The preposterous-minded were cowed—they thought
time would be given.

There was no need of a steed nor a lance to pursue
    them;
It was decreed their own deed, and not chance, should
    undo them.
The tares they had laughingly sown were ripe to the
    reaping,
The trust they had leagued to disown was removed
    from their keeping.
The eaters of other men's bread, the exempted from
    hardship,
The excusers of impotence fled, abdicating their ward-
    ship.
For the hate they had taught through the State brought
    the State no defender,
And it passed from the roll of the Nations in headlong
    surrender!

JUSTICE

OCTOBER, 1918

*A*CROSS *a world where all men grieve*
   And grieving strive the more,
     The great days range like tides and leave
Our dead on every shore.
Heavy the load we undergo,
   And our own hands prepare,
If we have parley with the foe,
   The load our sons must bear.

Before we loose the word
   That bids new worlds to birth,
Needs must we loosen first the sword
   Of Justice upon earth;
Or else all else is vain
   Since life on earth began,
And the spent world sinks back again
   Hopeless of God and Man.

A people and their King
   Through ancient sin grown strong,
Because they feared no reckoning
   Would set no bound to wrong;

JUSTICE

But now their hour is past,
  And we who bore it find
Evil Incarnate held at last
  To answer to mankind.

For agony and spoil
  Of nations beat to dust,
For poisoned air and tortured soil
  And cold, commanded lust,
And every secret woe
  The shuddering waters saw—
Willed and fulfilled by high and low—
  Let them relearn the Law.

That when the dooms are read,
  Not high nor low shall say:—
'My haughty or my humble head
  Has saved me in this day.'
That, till the end of time,
  Their remnant shall recall
Their fathers' old, confederate crime
  Availed them not at all.

That neither schools nor priests,
  Nor Kings may build again
A people with the heart of beasts
  Made wise concerning men.
Whereby our dead shall sleep
  In honour, unbetrayed,
And we in faith and honour keep
  That peace for which they paid.

THE MUSE AMONG THE MOTORS

CARMEN CIRCULARE

Horace.

D ELLIUS, that car which, so they say
    Jove's lightnings arm and Furies scourge—
    The terror of the Appian Way—
  Be slow to urge.

Though reckless Lydia bid thee fly
    And Telephus o'ertaking jeer,
Nay, sit and strongly occupy
    The lower gear.

They call, the road consenting 'Haste!'—
    Such as delight in dust collected—
Until arrives (I too have raced)
    The unexpected.

What ox not doomed to die alone,
    Or inauspicious hound shall bring
Thee 'twixt two kisses to the throne
    Of Hades' King.

I cannot tell; but, O pursue
    Far off thy Daunian carnage lest
The pallid corpse be mine to view
    At crowner's quest!

THE ADVERTISEMENT

(In the manner of the earlier English)

WHETHER to wander through straight streets
   strictly,
  Trimly by towns perfectly paved;
Or after office, as fitteth thy fancy,
Faring with friends far among fields;
There is none other equal in action
Sith she is silent, nimble, unnoisome,
Lordly of leather, gaudily gilded,
Burgeoning brightly in a brass bonnet,
Certain to steer well between wains.

THE JUSTICE'S TALE

Chaucer.

W ITH them there rode a lustie Engineere
Wel skilled to handel everich waie her geere,
He was soe wise ne man colde showe him
naught
And out of Paris was hys learnynge brought
Frontlings mid brazen wheeles and wandes he sat,
And on hys head he bare an leathern hat,
Hee was soe certaine of his gouvernance,
That, by the Roode he tooke everie chaunce.
For simple people and for lordlings eke
Hee wolde not bate a del but onlie squeeke
Behinde their backes on an horne hie
Until they crope into a piggestie.
He was more wood than bull in china-shoppe
And yet for cowes and dogges wolde hee stop,
Not out of Marcie but for preudence-sake—
Then hys dependaunce ever was hys brake.

TO A LADY, PERSUADING HER TO A CAR

Ben Jonson.

LOVE'S fiery chariot, Delia, take
  Which Vulcan wrought for Venus' sake,
  Wings shall not waft thee, but a flame
Hot as my heart—as nobly tame:
Lit by a spark, less bright, more wise
Than linkèd lightnings of thine eyes!
Seated and ready to be drawn,
Come not in muslins, lace or lawn,
But, for thy thrice imperial worth,
Take all the sables of the North,
With frozen diamonds belted on,
To face extreme Euroclydon.
Thus in our thund'ring toy we'll prove
Which is more blind, the Law or Love:
So may the jealous Gods prevent
Our fierce and uncontrouled descent!

THE PROGRESS OF THE SPARK (XVITH CIRCUIT)

Donne.

THIS spark now set, retarded, yet forbears
   To hold her light howeverso he swears
   That turns a metalled crank and, leather cloked,
With some small hammers tappeth hither and yon;
Peering as when she showeth and when is gone;
For wait he must till the vext power's evoked
That's one with the lightnings. Wait in the showers
    soaked
Or by the road-side sunned. She'll not progress.
Poor soul, here taught how great things may by less
Be stayed, to file contacts doth himself address!

THE BRAGGART

Mat. Prior.

PETROLIO, vaunting his Mercedes' power
Vows she can cover sixty miles an hour.
I tried the car of old and know she can,
But dare *he* ever do it?   Ask his man!

WHEN THE JOURNEY WAS INTENDED TO THE CITY'

Milton.

WHEN that with meat and drink they had ful-
        filled
        Not temperately but like him conceived
In monstrous jest at Meudon, whose regale
Stands for exemplar of Gargantuan greed,
In his own name supreme, they issued forth
Beneath new firmaments and stars astray
Circumvoluminant; nor had they felt
Neither the passage nor the sad effects
Of many cups partaken till that frost
Wrought on them hideous, and their mind deceived.
Thus choosing from a progeny of roads,
Which seemed but were not, one least reasonable,
Of purest moonlight figured on a wall,
Thither they urged their chariot whom that flint
Buttressed received, itself unscathed—not they.

TO MOTORISTS

Herrick.

SINCE ye distemper and defile
Sweet Here by the measured mile,
Nor aught on jocund highways heed
Except the evidence of speed;
And bear about your dreadful task
Faces beshrouded neath a mask,
Great goblin eyes and gluey hands
And souls enslaved to chains and bands,
Here shall no graver curse be said
Than, though y' are quick that ye are dead!

THE TOUR

Byron.

THIRTEEN as twelve my Murray always took.
  He was a publisher. The New Police
  Have neater ways of bringing men to book,
So Juan found himself before J. Ps.
Accused of storming through that placid nook
  At practically any pace you please.
The Dogberry, and the Waterbury made
It forty mile—five pounds. And Juan paid.

THE IDIOT BOY

Wordsworth.

HE wandered down the mountain-grade
    Beyond the speed assigned—
    A youth whom Justice often stayed
And generally fined.

He went alone, and none might know
    If he could drive or steer;
Now he is in the ditch, and O!
    The differential gear!

THE LANDAU

Praed.

THERE was a landau deep and wide,
    Cushioned for Sleep's own self to sit on—
    The glory of the country-side
From Tanner's End to Marlow Ditton.
John of the broad and brandied cheek
    (Well I recall its *eau-de-vie* hues!)
Drove staid Sir Ralph five days a week
    At speeds which we considered Jehu's.

But now poor John sleeps very sound,
    And neither hears nor smells the fuss
Of the young squire's nine hundred pound—
    Er—*Mors communis omnibus·*
And I who in my daily stroll
    Observe the reckless chauffeur crowd her—
Laudator temporis, extol
    The times before the Act allowed her.

CONTRADICTIONS

Longfellow.

THE drowsy carrier sways
  To the drowsy horses' tramp.
  His axles winnow the sprays
Of the hedge where the rabbit plays
  In the light of his single lamp.

He hears a horn behind
  And the jar of an angry bell.
A headlight strikes him blind
And a stench o'erpowers the wind
  Like a blast from the mouth of Hell.

He mends his swingle-bar,
  And loud his curses ring;
But a mother waiting afar
Hears the roar of the doctor's car
  Like the beat of an angel's wing!

So to the poet's mood
  Motor or carrier's van,
Properly understood,
Be neither evil nor good—
  Ormuzd nor Ahriman.

FASTNESS

Tennyson.

THIS is the end whereto men toiled
 Before thy coachman guessed his fate,
 How thou shouldst leave thy 'scutcheoned gate
On that new wheel which is the oiled—

To see the England Shakespeare saw
 (Oh, Earth, 'tis long since Shallow died!
 Yet by yon farrowed sow may hide
Some blue, deep minion of the Law)—

To range from Ashby-de-la-Zouch
 By Lyonesse to Locksley Hall
 Or haply, nearer home, appal
Thy father's sister's staid barouche.

THE BEGINNER

(After he has been extemporising on an instrument)

Browning.

L O! What is this that I make—sudden, supreme, un-
rehearsed—
This that my clutch in the crowd pressed at a
venture has raised?
Forward and onward I sprang when I thought (as I
ought) I reversed,
And a cab like a martagon opes and I sit in the
wreckage dazed.
And someone is taking my name, and the driver is
rending the air
With cries for my blood and my gold, and a snicker-
ing newsboy brings
My cap, wheel-pashed from the kerb. I must run her
home for repair,
Where she leers with her bonnet awry—flat on the
nether springs!

LADY GERALDINE'S HARDSHIP

Browning.

I TURNED—Heaven knows we women turn too
    much
  To broken reeds, mistaken so for pine
That shame forbids confession—a handle I turned
(The wrong one said the agent afterwards)
And so flung clean across your English street
Through the shrill-tinkling glass of the shop-front—
    paused.
Artemis mazed mid gauds to catch a man,
And piteous baby-caps and christening-gowns
The worse for being worn on the radiator!

  .   .   .   .

My cousin Romney judged me from the Bench:
Propounding one sleek forty-shillinged law
That takes no count of the Woman's Oversoul.
I should have entered, purred he, by the door—
The man's retort—the open obvious door,
But, since I chose not, he—not he—could change
The man's rule, not the Woman's, for the case.
Ten pounds or seven days . . . Just that . . .
    I paid!

THE BOTHER

Clough.

HASTILY Adam our driver swallowed a curse in
the darkness—
Petrol nigh at end and something wrong a
sprocket
Made him speer for the nearest town when lo! at the
crossways
Four blank letterless arms a virginal signpost ex-
tended.
'Look!' thundered Hugh the Radical. 'This is the
England we boast of—
Bland, white-bellied, obese but utterly useless for
business.
They are repainting the signs and have dropped the job
in the middle.
They are repainting the signs and traffic may halt till
they've done it,
Which is to say till the son of a gun of a local contractor,
Having laboriously wiped out every name for
Probably thirty miles round, be minded to finish his
labour!
Had not the fool the sense to paint in and paint out
together?'

THE BOTHER

Thus, not seeing his speech belied his Radical Gospel
(Which is to paint out the earth and then write 'Damn'
    on the shutter)
Hugh embroidered the theme imperially and stretched
    it
From some borough in Wales through our Australian
    possessions,
Making himself, reformer wise, a bit of a nuisance
Till, with the help of Adam, we cast him out on the
    landscape.

THE DYING CHAUFFEUR

Adam Lindsay Gordon.

WHEEL me gently to the garage, since my car
and I must part—
 No more for me the record and the run.
That cursed left-hand cylinder the doctors call my
heart
 Is pinking past redemption—I am done!
They'll never strike a mixture that'll help me pull my
load.
 My gears are stripped—I cannot set my brakes.
I am entered for the finals down the timeless untimed
Road
 To the Maker of the makers of all makes!

THE INVENTOR

Emerson.

TIME and Space decreed his lot
    But little Man was quick to note
    When Time and Space said Man might not,
Bravely he answered, 'Nay—I mote.'

I looked on old New England.
    Time and Space stood fast
Men built altars to Distance
    At every mile they passed.

Yet sleek with oil, a Force was hid
    Making mock of all they did
Ready at the opening hour
To yield up to Prometheus
The secular and well-drilled Power
The Gods secreted thus.

And over high Wantastiquet
Emulous my lightnings ran,
Unregarded but afret,
To fall in with my plan.

I beheld two Ministries
　　One of Air and one of Earth—
At a thought I married these,
　　And my New Age came to birth.

For rarely my Purpose errs
　　Though oft it seemed to pause
And rods and cylinders
　　Obey my planets' laws.

Oil I drew from the well
　　And Franklin's spark from its blue,—
Time and Distance fell
　　And Man went forth anew.

On the prairie and on the street
　　So long as my chariots roll
I bind wings to Adam's feet,
　　And presently to his soul.

THE SONG OF THE MOTOR

(Author Unknown.)

YOU mustn t groom an Arab with a file.
    You hadn't ought to tension-spring a mule.
    You couldn't push a Brumby fifty mile
And drop him in a boiler-shed to cool.
I'll sling you through six counties in a day
    I'll hike you up a grade of one in ten.
I'm Duty, Law and Order under way,
    I'm the Mentor of banana-fingered men.
I will make you know your left hand from your right.
    I will teach you not to drink about your biz!
I'm the only temperance advocate in sight!
    I am all the Education Act there is!

THE MARRED DRIVES OF WINDSOR

ACT II—SCENE III

SCENE: *The Boar's Head Tavern in Eastcheap.*
[Enter FALSTAFF, *habited as a motorist.*

FALSTAFF.   Here's all at end between us, or I'll never taste sack again. Prince or no Prince, I'll not ride with him to Coventry on the hinder parts of a carbonadoed stink, not though he call her all the car in Christendom. Sack! Sack! Sack!

HOSTESS.   I spied her out of the lattice. A fizzled and a groaned and a shook from the bones out, Sir John, and a ran on her own impulsidges back and forth o' Chepe, and I knew that there was but one way to it when I saw them fighting at the handles. She died of a taking of pure wind on the heart, and they be about her body now with tongs. A marvellous searching perfume, Sir John!

FALSTAFF.   He hath called me ribs; he hath called me tallow. There is no name in the extremer oiliness of comparison which I have not borne meekly. But to go masked at midday; to wrap my belly in an horse-

138

hide cloak of ten thousand buttons till I looked like a mushroomed dunghill; to be smoked over burnt oils; to be enseamed, moreover, with intolerable greases; and thus scented, thus habited, thus vizarded to leap out—for I leaped, mark you . . . Another cup of sack! But here's vengeance for my case! These eyes have seen the Lord's Anointed on his knees in Chepe, foining with the key of Shrewsbury Castle, which Poins had bent to the very crook of Nym's theftuous elbow, to wake the dumb devil in the guts of her. 'Sweet Hal,' said I, 'Are all horses sold out of England, that thou must kneel before the lieges to any petrol-piddling turnspit?' Then he, Poins and Bardolph, whose nose blanched with sheer envy of her bodywork, begged a shoulder of me to thrust her into some alley, the street being full of Ephesians of the old church. Whereat I—

[*Enter* PRINCE *and* FLUELLEN.

PRINCE. Whereat thou, hearing her once or twice tenderly backfire—

FALSTAFF. Heaven forgive thee, Hal! She thundered and lightened a full half-hour, so that Jove himself could not have bettered the instruction. There's a pit beneath her now, which she blew out of thy father's highway the while I watched, where Sackerson could stand to six dogs.

PRINCE. Hearing, I say, her gentle outcry against

139

Poins' mishandling, thou didst flee up Chepe calling upon the Sheriff's watch for a red flag.

FALSTAFF. I? Call me Jack if I were not jack to each of her wheels in turn till I am stamped like a butter-pat with the imprint of her underpinnings. *I* seek a red flag?

PRINCE. Ay, roaring like a bull.

FALSTAFF. Groans, Hal, groans—such as Atlas heaved. But she overbore me at the last. Why hast thou left her? Faugh, that a King's son should ever reek like a smutty-wicked lamp upon the wrong side of morning!

PRINCE. There was Bardolph in the buckbasket behind, nosing fearfully overside like a full-wattled turkey-poult from Norfolk. There was Poins upon his belly beneath her, thrice steeped in pure plumbago, most despairfully clanking of chains like the devil in Brug's Hall window; and there were some four thousand 'prentices at her tail, crying, 'What ho!' and that she bumped. Methought 'twas no place for my father's son.

FALSTAFF. Take any man's horses and hale her to bed. The laws of England are at thy commandment, that the Heir should not be made a common stink in the nostrils of the lieges.

PRINCE. She'd not stir for all Apollo's team—not though Phaeton himself, drunk with nec-

140

tar, lashed 'em stark mad. Poor Phaeton!

HOSTESS. A was a King's son, was a not, and a came to's end by keeping o' bad company.

FALSTAFF. No more than a little horseflesh. I tell thee, Hal, this England of ours has never looked up since the nobles fell to puking over oil-buckets by the side of leather-jerkined Walloons.

PRINCE. He that drives me now is French as our princely cousin.

FALSTAFF. Dumain? Hang him for a pestilent, poke-eyed, chicken-chopping, hump-backed, leather-hatted, muffle-gloved ape! He hath been fined as often as he hath broken down; and that is at every tavern 'twixt here and York. Dumain! He's the most notorious widow-maker on the Windsor road. His mother was a corn-cutter at Ypres, and his father a barber at Rouen, by which beastly conjunction he rightly draws every infirmity that damns him in his trade. He cuts corners niggardly and upon the wrong side. *Item:* He'll look behind him after a likely wench in the hottest press of Holborn, though he skid into the kennel for it. *Item:* He depends upon his brake to save him at need—a death-bed repentance, Hal, as hath been proved ere this, since grace is uncertain. *Item:* He is too proud to clean the body of her, but leaves the care of that which should be the very cote-armour of his mechanic knighthood to an unheedful ostler. Thus, at last, he comes to overlook even the oiling; and so it falls that she's where she must be, and not where thou wouldst have her. Ay, laugh if thou wilt, Hal, but a round worthy knight need not fire himself through three baronies in eight hours to know the very essence of the petard that hoists him. Dumain will one day clutch thee into Hell upon the first or lesser speed.

PRINCE. Strange that clear knowledge should so long outlive mere nerve! I'll dub Dumain knight when I come to the throne, if he be not hanged first for murder on the highway. 'Twill save the state a pension.

FALSTAFF. So the lean vice goes ever before the solid virtue.

[Confused noises without.
What riot's afoot now?

FLUELLEN. Riots, look you, by my vizaments, make one noise, but murders, another. There's riots in Monmouth; but, by my vizaments, look you, there's murders in Chepe. Pabes and old 'oomen—they howl so tamnably.

FALSTAFF. Rebellion rather! Half London's calling on thy name, Hal, and half on thy father's. Well, if it be successful, forget not who was promised the reversion of the Chief Justiceship. Ha! Unquestioned rebellion, if broken crowns signify aught.

[Enter HERALDS, *wounded.*

HERALDS.   Most gracious lord, the car that bore thy
                state,
             Too long neglected and adjudged acold,
             Hath, without warning or advertisement,
             Risen refreshed from her supposed stand
             In unattended revolution.

PRINCE.   This it is to be a King's son! That a
             pitiful twelve-horse touring-car cannot jar
             off her brakes but they must rehearse it
             me in damnable heroics. Your pleasure,
             gentlemen?

HERALDS.   The blood upon our boltered brow attests
             'Twas Bardolph's art that waked her,
                whereat she
             Skipped thunderously before our mazed
                eyes
             Drew out o'er several lieges (all with God!),
             Battered a house or so to laths, and now
             Fumes on her side in Holborn. Please
                you come!

PRINCE.   Anon! Seek each a physician according
             to his needs and revenues. I'll be with
             you anon. [*To* FALSTAFF.] The third in
             three weeks! These whoreson German
             clock-cases no sooner dint an honest
             English paving-stone than they inconti-
             nent lay their entrails on the street. Five
             hundred and seventy pounds! I'll out
             and pawn the Duchy!

HERALDS.   The Lord Chief Justice waits thy princely
                will,
             In thy dread father's Court at West-
                minster.

FALSTAFF.   Glasses, Doll! We'll drink to his de-
             liverance. A Star Chamber matter, Hal
             —a Star Chamber matter!

HERALDS.   You, too, Sir John as party to these broils.
             And breakings-forth, in like attainder stand
             For judgment; wherein fail not at your
             peril!

FALSTAFF.   I do remember now to have had some
             dealings with this same Chief Justice. An
             old feeble man, drawn abroad in a cart,
             by horses. We must enlighten—enlighten
             him, Hal.

                                        EXEUNT.

THE MARRED DRIVES OF WINDSOR

Act III—Scene I

ARGUMENT: PRINCE HENRY, POINS, FLUELLEN, NYM, *and* SIR JOHN, FALSTAFF, (BARDOLPH *having escaped*) *are charged, on* DOGBERRY'S *evidence, before the Lord Chief Justice at Westminster, with exceeding the speed limit and leaving their car unattended in the street.* PORTIA *defends them.* Mr. Justice SHALLOW *has been accommodated with a seat on the Bench.*

PRINCE. Where's our red rear-lamp? Where's Bardolph?

POINS. Shining over Southwark if he be not puffed out by now. He ran when the watch came. The Chief Justice looks sourly. Is any appointed to speak for us, Hal?

PRINCE. Thy notorious innocence, my known virtue, and, if these fail, Sir John's big belly. I have fed my father's Exchequer here twice since Easter.

CHIEF JUSTICE. Intemperate, rash, and ill-advised men— Yoke-fellows at unsavoury enterprise— Harry, and you, Sir John, stand forth for sentence!

FLUELLEN. Put—put there is no indictment, dis charged upon us yet! To pronounc sentences, look you, pefore the indict ments is discharged is ropperies and oppressions.

NYM. Ay, that's the humour of it. When the cry Budget we must cry mum.

FALSTAFF. Cram the Welsh flannel down his own throat, or we are imprisoned after the fine I know the Chief Justice is sick of me.

SHALLOW. [*To* CHIEF JUSTICE.] My lord, my lord if you suffer yond fat knight to talk, he'l cozen the teeth out of your lordship's head while his serving-man steals the steeped crust you'd mumble to. I lent him thousand pounds, my lord.

FALSTAFF. I deny it not. For the which I promised thee advancement. And art thou no now visibly next the Chief Justice him self?

SHALLOW. Not on my merits, Sir John. I sit here simple of courtesy as visiting-justice. I'd do as much for my lord if he came to Gloucestershire, 'faith!

FALSTAFF. Shallow! Shallow! I say I gave thee occasion and opportunity to rise. Promo tion is in thy hands. [*To* CHIEF JUSTICE.] Have a care, my lord! He fingers his dagger already.

SHALLOW. My dagger? My ink-horn, la! I'll sit further off. I told you how he'd talk, my lord. But I'll sit further off. My dagger, 'faith!

THE MARRED DRIVES OF WINDSOR

CHIEF JUSTICE. Sir John! Sir John! The license of inveterate humour overstretched rends like an outworn garment—with like shame to the enduer. Answer me roundly, what defence make you to the charge you have run through Chepe at ten leagues the hour?

FALSTAFF. Roundly, my lord, my shape—my evident shape.

CHIEF JUSTICE. But 'tis so charged. and will be so witnessed.

DOGBERRY. Yes, and by one that hath a stopped watch and everything forsworn about him. Write it down fifteen leagues, my lord.

PRINCE. [*To* CHIEF JUSTICE.] We knights of the road have ever been fair quarry for your knights of the post to bind to, but this passes endurance. We left our car, my lord, extinct and combust in the kennel, whilst we sought an engineer to hoist her. In which stay would she have continued, but for the prying vulgar who found on her some handle to their curiosity, which, doubtless, they turned. For, in such a car as this——

CHIEF JUSTICE. In such a car as this
The enfranchised 'prentices of London quash
Our harmless babes and necessary wives

147

At morning to the sound of Sabbath bells
Through panicked Huntingdon.

PORTIA.
In such a car as this,
Slides young Desire athwart the mountain-tops,
Drinking the airs that part him from his dear
'Twixt Berwick and Glamorgan.

CHIEF
JUSTICE.
In such a car as this
The lecherous Israelite to Brighthelmstone
Convoys his Jessica.

PORTIA.
In such a car as this,
The lean chirurgeon burns the midnight oil
Impetuous over England. Where his lamp
Strikes pale the hedgerow, all affrighted fays,
Their misty revels in the dew divulged,
Flee to the coney's burrow, or divide
His antre with the squirrel—whom that ministrant
Marks not, his eyes being bent to thrid the dark,
Indifferent beneath the morning-star,
To the poor cot that summoned him, and the life—
An hour-old, mother-naked life, scarce held
By the wan midwife but it yerks and squeaks
Batlike, and batlike, would to the void again.

	This he forbids, and yet not he whose art, His car unaiding, else had ne'er o'erleaped The largess of a county in an hour.
SHALLOW.	Neat, faith, la! For how a brace of twins now the far side Cotsall, of a snowy night, my lord.
FALSTAFF.	A pregnant wit. Which of thy misdeeds, Hal, hath raised this angel to help us? I'll ask Doll.
PRINCE.	Peace, Dunghill, peace! She was never of Doll's company.
PORTIA.	And I charge you, my lord, if ever need, Extreme and urgent need, hath visited you, Or, in the unprobeable decrees of Time, May visit and masterfully constrain, think well Ere your abhorrence of new enginery Seal up the avenues of mercy here!
CHIEF JUSTICE.	I sealed no avenues. They sealed the King's (Albeit it was called Northumberland) With hellish engines drawn across the street In an opposed and desperate barrier Unto the lieges' progress.
PORTIA.	Not by their will, or their intent, my lord! It was a passing humour of the car— Gusty incontinence, which overlooked, As unregard oft cows pretension, May well not chance again.

CHIEF JUSTICE.	But if it chance?
PORTIA.	If the deep-brooding vault of Heaven retain
	Memory and record of miracle
	Vouchsafed, like this your prayed-for mercy, once,
	And, in default of quail, rain from her gate
	Heaven's sweetest choristers—then it may fall,
	But not till then!
FLUELLEN.	Put—put—look you, she is telling the old shentlemans to wait till the sky shall rain larks. It is open contempts of Courts!
NYM.	Ay, there's humours in them all. But I think the old man's humour is sweeter.
CHIEF JUSTICE.	Yet, bating miracle, how if mercy breed
	Not gratitude, but livelier insolence,
	And through my softened verdict after-years
	Grow bold to break the law? How if our England—
	Loverly, temperate, the midmost close of peace—
	Dissolve in dust and oils along the green,
	Till sickened memory conceive no minute
	Unharried, unpollutable, unhooted?
	If I loose these, what do I loose on England?
PORTIA.	Too late! Too late! That babe is viable!
	The hour we dread o'ertops us while we wonder,

Not asking sufferance but imposing change
Most multitudinously.   Hark, it sings i'
the wind!

ARIEL.   [*Invisible—sings:*]
Where the car slips there slip I—
In a sunbeam's path I lie!
There I crouch while crowds do cry,
After somersaults muddily!
Where I lie, where I lie, shall I live now
Under the bonnet that bangs on my brow?

FALSTAFF.   [*To* PRINCE.]
The Chief Justice is mazed by the fairies.
He hath great motions towards virtue.
He'll let us go.

CHIEF
JUSTICE.   Ourselves have snuffed some savour of
these changes,
And more our horses who, poor winkered
fools,
Hearing their dooms outstrip them,
swerve aside
And pole the all-shattered house-fronts.
We ourselves
Of purpose to repair to Westminster,
Infirmity and age consenting, signalled
From her hot lair an horseless chariot
Which, in the recorded twelfth part of an
hour
Bore our inviolate ermines half a league.
It is, and woe it is, the chill refuge,
The lean, unenvied privilege of age,
To meet new changes with old courtesy,

Not as averting change but sparing souls
Worn weak, and bodies extenuate, with
the years
That heed nor never heeded. Set them
free.
What was has been, and what will be,
must be!

THE END.